$\frac{1}{2} \times \frac{3}{4} = \frac{3}{8}$

$1\frac{1}{8}$

6.25
3.16
―――
9.41

Bond
No.1 for exam success

Maths and Non-verbal Reasoning

10 Minute Tests

CEM (Durham University)

10–11⁺ years

3366785
+ 12329423
―――――――
15665208

3336785
12329423
―――――――
15666208

OXFORD
UNIVERSITY PRESS

Test 1: Non-verbal Reasoning

Test time: 0 5 10 minutes

Which pattern completes the grid? Underline the correct answer.

1    a   b   c   d   e

2    a   b   c   d   e

3   a   b   c   d   e

4   a   b   c   d   e

There is a set of pictures on the left with a missing picture shown by a question mark. Underline the correct option from the right to complete the set.

5  ?
   a   b   c   d   e

6  ?
   a   b   c   d   e

7   ?
   a   b   c   d   e

Which cube cannot be made from the given net? Underline the correct answer.

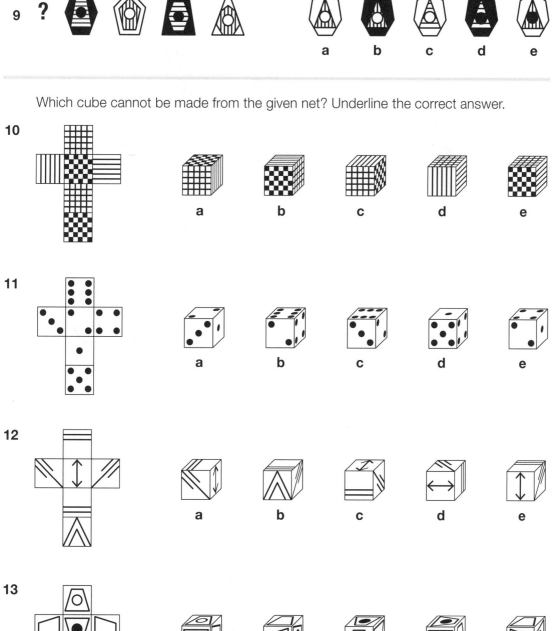

Test 2: Data

This chart shows the test results for Year 5 and Year 6 tests over four years.
Use the chart to answer the following questions.

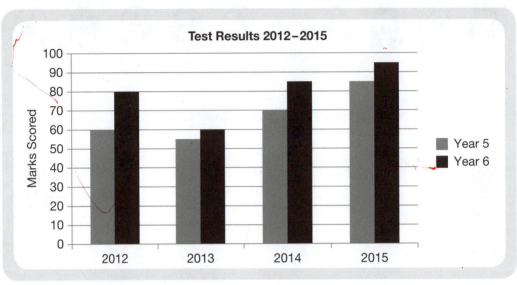

1 What is the mean score for Year 6? _80_

2 What is the range including both year groups? _~~70~~_

3 What is the median score including both year groups? _75_

4 How many more marks did Year 6 score than Year 5? _50_

Here is a section of a bus timetable. Use it to answer the following questions.

	Bus 1	Bus 2	Bus 1	Bus 2	Bus 1
Blossomfield	11:35	11:58	12:35	12:56	13:35
Widney Lane		12:15		13:13	
Stratford Road	11:47		12:47		13:47
Hillfield Park	12:04		13:04		14:04
Widney Manor	12:14	12:35	13:14	13:33	14:14
Prince's Way	12:25	12:46	13:25	13:44	14:25

5 I leave Blossomfield at 11:35, get off at Widney Manor and spend one and a half hours before catching the next bus to Prince's Way. At what time do I reach Prince's Way?   _14:25_ [1]

6 How long does it take to travel from Stratford Road to Prince's Way?   _38 mins_ [1]

7 I need to get to Widney Manor by 1 p.m. What is the latest time that I can leave Blossomfield to get there on time?   _11:58_ [1]

8 The two buses are running on a circular route. How long does it take to get from Prince's Way back to Blossomfield?   _10 mins_ [1]

This table shows the most popular items sold by the Happy Snack Bar. Use the table to answer the following questions.

Happy Snack Bar	Sugar	Salt	Fat	Calories	Fibre
Crunchy Carrot Sticks	5.8 g	0.08 g	0	34	2.4 g
Fresh Fruit Bag	26 g	0.08 g	0	126	6.1 g
Pick & Mix Salad	28 g	0.13 g	0.9 g	144	7.2 g
Large Chilli Veggie Wrap	36 g	1.5 g	2.2 g	572	14 g
Grilled Chicken With Salad	40 g	2.3 g	2.6 g	695	16 g
Merry Berry Muffin	38 g	1.4 g	2.7 g	548	9 g

9 If 1 teaspoon of sugar is 4 g, how many teaspoons of sugar are there in a grilled chicken with salad meal?   _~~8~~ 10_ [1]

10 Which snack has 7 teaspoons of sugar in it?   [1]

Pick and mix salad

11 If I ate a Fresh Fruit Bag and a Large Chilli Veggie Wrap, how many calories would I eat?   _698_ [1]

12 If a 10-year-old child should consume no more than 5 g of salt a day, what percentage of the total daily amount would a Large Chilli Veggie Wrap and a Merry Berry Muffin be?   _58%_ [2]

Total 13

Test 3: Word Problems

Samson decides to paint glass baubles to sell at the Winter Fair. He needs to buy ten bottles of glass paint and sees the following special offers:

SYED'S SALE
All bottles of **GLASS PAINT**
now
£6.99
a bottle

BARTOSZ'S BARGAINS
Glass paint
£8.20 a bottle
with 15% discount off the total order

OZZY'S OFFERS
Glass paint
£9.85
Buy **TWO** and receive the **THIRD** bottle **FREE!**

1 What is the cheapest price for ten bottles of glass paint? _____ [3]

2 Samson works out that each painted bauble costs £1.15 to make. He sells the baubles for £3.99 each. If Samson sells 50 baubles, how much profit does he make?   £14.20 [2]

Brooke and her friends are raising money by making friendship bands. They charge £3.50 per band. Brooke can make six bands per hour. Zara can make two more per hour than Brooke. Sophia can make half the number that Zara can per hour, which is one fewer per hour than Molly can make.

3 How long does it take Molly to make 15 friendship bands?   3 hours [1]

4 The girls decide to raise £1000 for charity. If they each make their maximum number of friendship bands per hour, how many complete hours do they need to work before they have raised enough money?   _____ [3]

Michael bakes 500 doughnuts. Every third doughnut has white icing. Every fifth doughnut has chocolate sprinkles. Every sixth doughnut is filled with custard.

5 How many doughnuts will have white icing on them and will also be filled with custard?   16 [2]

6 How many doughnuts will have both white icing and chocolate sprinkles on them?   _____ [2]

Total [13]

Test 4: Word Problems

1. Geno has some 1 cm cubes. He has a box with sides 10 cm × 6 cm × 5 cm. How many of the cubes will fit into the box? _300 cm²_

2. Inside each 1 cm cube Geno has placed three beads. How many beads will there be in the box? _900_

3. Each bead costs Geno 8p. How much do the bead contents of the box cost in total? _72.88p_

900 p
7288

Jodie makes a pattern using circles and squares. She extends the pattern each time and puts the following mathematical equations into her patterns:

Pattern 1
$2 + 1^2 = 3$

Pattern 2
$3 + 2^2 = 7$

Pattern 3
$4 + 3^2 = 13$

Pattern 4
$5 + 4^2 = 21$

6+5 7+6 8+7 9+8 10+9
11+10

4. What would be the answer for pattern 11? _$11 + 10^2 = 110$_

5. What would be the answer for pattern 51? _82755_

6. Which pattern would give the answer 157? _$13 + 12^2$_

Jon buys some glow sticks and modelling balloons for a party. There are 25 glow sticks in a box and Jon buys three boxes. The modelling balloons cost 4p each and Jon buys 140 of them. Jon pays for the items with two £20 notes and gets £8.15 change.

7. How much are the glow sticks each? _____

8. If Jon is offered a 20% discount on the modelling balloons, how much change would he now get from the two £20 notes? _____

9. Jon finds that one in every 15 glow sticks does not work. How many of the total number do not work? _____

Test 5: **Mixed**

Which pattern completes the grid? Underline the correct answer.

1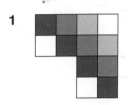
                                               a   b   c   d   e

2
                                               a   b   c   d   e

3
                                               a   b   c   d   e

This chart shows the points scored by Overbury School sports teams. Use the chart to answer the following questions.

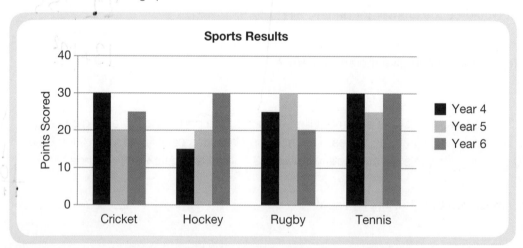

4 What was the mean score for Year 4? Underline the correct answer.

    a 25   **b** 100   **c** 20   **d** 50   **e** 30

5 Which **TWO** sports scored the same number of points in total? Underline **TWO** answers.

    a Cricket   **b** Hockey   **c** Rugby   **d** Tennis

6 Which score was the mode? Underline the correct answer.

   a 15   b 20   c 25   d 30   e 35

Mrs Skidmore's Stationery Shop has these items to sell. Underline the correct answer for each of the questions below.

Crayons £3.75
Notebook £2.69
Pencil 75p
Pen £1.19
Envelopes £2.50
Sketch Pad £4.25

7 Kishor buys three pens, three pencils, a packet of crayons, a notebook and a sketch pad. He pays with a £20 note. How much change does he receive?

   a £3.14   b £3.24   c £3.49   d £3.94   e £7.54

8 Mrs Skidmore decides to reduce the price of all of her items by 20%. Yuwei decides to buy two packs of envelopes and two pencils. How much does she pay?

   a £5.00   b £5.10   c £5.20   d £5.30   e £5.40

9 Pens come in packs of 12 with 50 packs in a box. There are 30 boxes in a pallet and Mrs Skidmore buys two pallets. How many pens does she buy?

   a 12   b 50   c 600   d 18 000   e 36 000

At Bridgenorth market there are 80 stalls divided into those selling food, those selling antiques and the rest selling other items. There are 42 stalls selling food or antiques. There are 56 selling antiques or other items. Underline the correct answer for each of the questions below.

10 How many stalls sell food?

   a 18   b 24   c 38   d 56   e 80

11 How many stalls sell antiques?

   a 18   b 24   c 38   d 56   e 80

12 How many stalls sell other items?

   a 18   b 24   c 38   d 56   e 80

Time for a break! ★ *Go to Puzzle Page 72* →

Test 6: **Non-verbal Reasoning**

Test time: 0 — 5 — 10 minutes

There is a set of pictures on the left with a missing picture shown by a question mark. Underline the correct option from the right to complete the set.

1   ?
                                                  a   b   c   d   e

2 ?
                                                  a   b   c   d   e

3 ? **V F M X**   **Z K Y T I**
                                                a   b   c   d   e

4 ?
                                                a   b   c   d   e

Which cube cannot be made from the given net? Underline the correct answer.

5
                                        a   b   c   d   e

6
                                        a   b   c   d   e

7

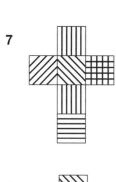

                         a   b   c   d   e

8

                         a   b   c   d   e

Which pattern completes the grid? Underline the correct answer.

9

                         a   b   c   d   e

10

                         a   b   c   d   e

11

                         a   b   c   d   e

12

                         a   b   c   d   e

Test 7: **Data**

480 pupils at St John's School were asked about their favourite films. This pie chart shows the results. Use the pie chart to answer the following questions.

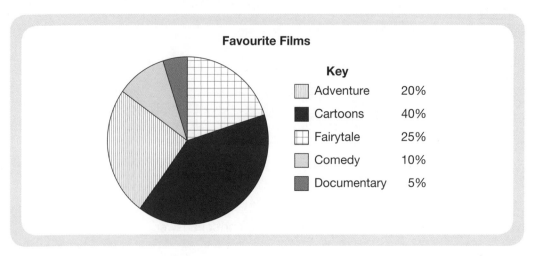

1 How many children prefer adventure films?   96

2 How many children prefer cartoons?   192

3 Which **TWO** film types were chosen by half the children as their favourite?
   Comedy + Cartoons

In this Venn diagram, each section has been labelled from A to G. Look at the following questions and decide in which section of the diagram each number would fit.

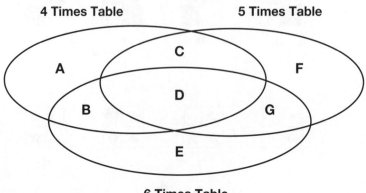

4 Where would the number 20 fit? __C__

5 Where would the number 60 fit? __D__

6 Where would the number 96 fit? __B__

7 Where would the number 110 fit? __F__

Ashfordington Village kept a record of all of the children born over a decade. On this chart they plotted how many girls and how many boys were born. Use the chart to answer the following questions.

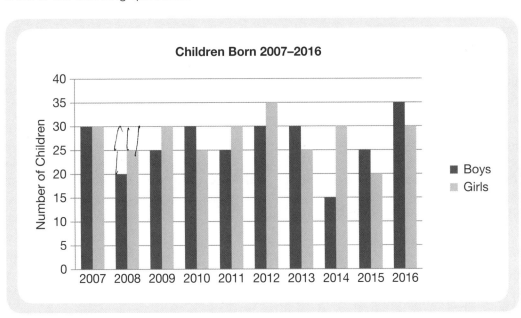

8 In what year were the highest number of girls born? __2012__

9 In what year were the highest number of boys born? __2016__

10 In what year were an equal number of girls and boys born? __2007__

11 How many children in total were born over the decade? __545__

Test 8: Word Problems

Test time: 0 — 5 — 10 minutes

Rose places 40 counters into a bag. $\frac{1}{4}$ of the counters are white, $\frac{3}{10}$ are yellow and the rest are blue. Underline the correct answer for each question.

1. How many counters are either white or blue?

   a 10   b 16   c 20   d 28   e 30

2. What percentage of the counters are either yellow or white?

   a 25%   b 26%   c 30%   d 55%   e 75%

3. What fraction of the counters are either yellow or blue?

   a $\frac{1}{2}$ b $\frac{3}{5}$ c $\frac{3}{4}$ d $\frac{4}{5}$ e $\frac{9}{10}$

Hamish has bought a box to hold presents for his mum. The box measures 22 cm wide, 30 cm high and 25 cm deep. He also buys a 5 m roll of wrapping paper to wrap up the box. Underline the correct answer for each question.

4. What is the volume of the box?

   a 660 cm³   b 750 cm³   c 1650 cm³   d 1750 cm³   e 16500 cm³

5. What is the surface area of the box?

   a 1960 cm²   b 2940 cm²   c 3920 cm²   d 16500 cm²   e 33000 cm²

6. If the wrapping paper costs £8.00 a roll, how much does 1 m cost?

   a 15p   b 16p   c £1.58   d £1.60   e £7.99

My map has a scale of 1 : 500 000. Underline the correct answer for each question.

7. I am travelling from my house to the airport, which is a distance of 30 km. How many centimetres on the map will this be?

   a 5 cm   b 6 cm   c 8 cm   d 10 cm   e 15 cm

8. If I travel at 65 km per hour, how many minutes will it take for me to drive to the airport from my house to the nearest minute?

   a 26   b 27   c 28   d 29   e 30

Total 11

Test 9: Word Problems

Beth has three identical pizzas. Ravi eats $\frac{2}{3}$ of a pizza. Charlie eats $\frac{3}{4}$ of a pizza. Nadia eats $\frac{1}{2}$ of a pizza and Selina eats $\frac{5}{6}$ of a pizza. Beth eats the remaining pizza.

1 How much pizza does Beth eat? _____

2 Who eats the largest amount of pizza? _____

3 Who eats the least amount of pizza? _____

Arsene looks at the 120 books on his bookshelf. He realises that $\frac{1}{2}$ of them are paperback and the remainder are hardback. He notices that in both types of book 40% of them are factual and the remainder are fiction. He sees that of the fiction books, 25% of them are by his favourite author.

4 How many books are factual paperbacks? _____

5 How many books are hardback and by his favourite author? _____

6 How many books are paperback and fiction, but not by his favourite author? _____

Pascha buys 17 televisions costing £389 each. When he sells them in his online shop, he adds on 30%. When he sells them in his town centre shop, he adds on 40%.

7 If Pascha could sell all of the televisions online, how much profit would he make? Remember to take off what Pascha paid for the televisions. _____

8 If Pascha could sell all of the televisions in his town centre shop, how much additional profit would he make compared to selling them online? _____

Total 17

Test 10: **Mixed**

We surveyed 280 teenagers and asked each of them what their favourite hobby was. This pie chart shows the results. Use the chart to answer the following questions.

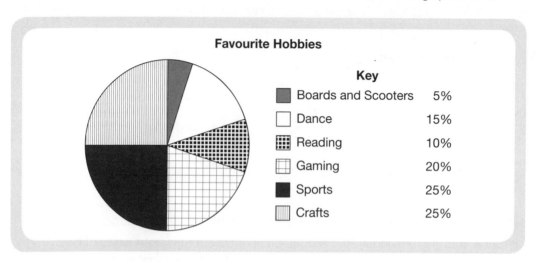

1 How many teenagers prefer Gaming? _____

2 How many teenagers prefer Boards and Scooters? _____

3 Write the fraction, in its simplest form, of teenagers who prefer Crafts or Reading. _____

4 How many teenagers prefer either Dance or Sports? _____

There is a set of pictures on the left with a missing picture shown by a question mark. Underline the correct option from the right to complete the set.

5
                                                                          a   b   c   d   e

6
                                                                          a   b   c   d   e

Which cube cannot be made from the given net? Underline the correct answer.

7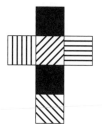

                                  a   b   c   d   e

8 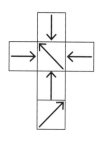

                                  a   b   c   d   e

Luigi cooks 12 pizzas. He cuts up each pizza into ten slices and piles them on a plate to be shared among his friends.

9 Gratziano eats six slices of pizza. Write the fraction of pizza that is left, in its simplest form. _____

10 Gratziano then passes four slices of pizza to Geno. Write the fraction of pizza now left, in its simplest form. _____

11 Another 38 slices of pizza were eaten. What percentage of pizza is left? _____

12 Write what fraction of pizza has been eaten in total, in its simplest form. _____

Test 11: Non-verbal Reasoning

Which pattern on the right completes the second pair in the same way as the first pair? Underline the correct answer.

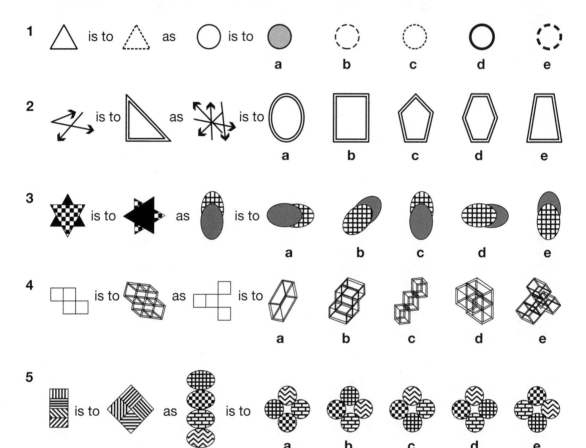

Which shape on the right is a 3D rotation of the shape on the left? Underline the correct answer.

Example:

            a   b   <u>c</u>   d   e

6
            a   b   c   d   e

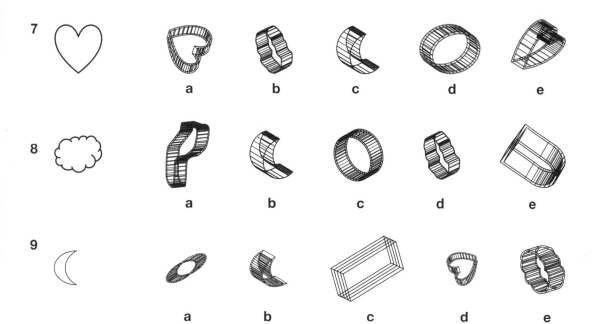

Which pattern completes the grid? Underline the correct answer.

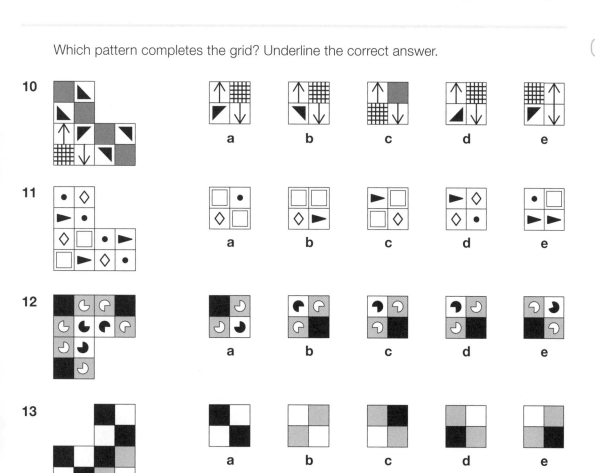

Test 12: Sequences

Continue these sequences.

1. 1234 1381 1528 1675 1822 _____ _____

2. 9513 9384 9255 9126 8997 _____ _____

3. −4500 −4450 −4400 −4350 −4300 _____ _____

Complete these sequences.

4. $\frac{1}{6}$ $\frac{1}{3}$ _____ $\frac{2}{3}$ $\frac{5}{6}$ _____ $1\frac{1}{6}$

5. 1 _____ $\frac{7}{9}$ $\frac{2}{3}$ _____ $\frac{4}{9}$ $\frac{1}{3}$

6. _____ $6\frac{1}{2}$ $7\frac{3}{4}$ _____ $10\frac{1}{4}$ $11\frac{1}{2}$ $12\frac{3}{4}$

Continue these sequences.

7. 2147 214.7 21.47 2.147 0.2147 _____ _____

8. −0.29 −0.17 −0.05 0.07 0.19 0.31 _____ _____

9. 12.67 10.68 8.69 6.70 4.71 _____ _____

Complete these sequences.

10. 1 3 _____ 27 _____ 243 729

11. _____ 4032 2016 1008 _____ 252 126

12. 6 _____ 12 _____ 144 720 4320

Test 13: Word Problems

Test time: 0 — 5 — 10 minutes

In an office there are four times as many women as men. There are seven times more non-managers than managers. There are 640 people working in the office. One in eight people did not go to university.

1 How many people went to university? _____ [1]

2 How many people are likely to be men and did not go to university? _____ [1]

3 How many people are likely to be women managers who went to university? _____ [2]

Kishor and his friends like to make origami animals. Kishor can make six animals per hour, which is two more per hour than Bharani. Bharani does one more per hour than Gnanan who makes half as many origami animals as Thanikai.

4 How many origami animals does Gnanan make? _____ [1]

5 Which two boys make the same number of animals per hour? _____ [1]

6 If all of the boys work for three hours, how many origami animals are made? _____ [2]

In St John's school there are 20 rooms that need cleaning. It takes four cleaners two hours each school day to clean all of the rooms.

7 How long does each room take to clean? _____ [2]

8 If two cleaners turn up, how long does it take them to clean? _____ [1]

9 If six cleaners turn up, how long does it take them to clean? _____ [2]

10 If the cleaning takes 48 minutes, how many cleaners are there? _____ [2]

Total [15]

Test 14: **Data**

Test time: 0 — 5 — 10 minutes

Yesterday Michael and Zara each recorded how busy they were during the day. Use the chart to answer the following questions. Underline the correct answer.

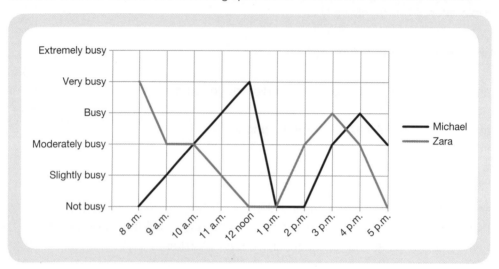

1 At what time was Michael the busiest?

  a 8 a.m.   **b** 10 a.m.   **c** 12 noon   **d** 3 p.m.   **e** 5 p.m.

2 At what time was Zara the busiest?

  a 8 a.m.   **b** 10 a.m.   **c** 12 noon   **d** 3 p.m.   **e** 5 p.m.

3 At what time did Michael stop for lunch?

  a 11 a.m.   **b** 12 noon   **c** 1 p.m.   **d** 2 p.m.   **e** 3 p.m.

4 At what time did Zara stop for lunch?

  a 11 a.m.   **b** 12 noon   **c** 1 p.m.   **d** 2 p.m.   **e** 3 p.m.

This table shows the village dog show results. There were 100 points shared between the five categories. Use the table to answer the following questions. Underline the correct answer.

	Looks	Behaviour	Agility	Obedience	Gait
Terriers	$\frac{18}{20}$	$\frac{13}{20}$	$\frac{15}{20}$	$\frac{15}{20}$	$\frac{19}{20}$
Working Dogs	$\frac{16}{20}$	$\frac{13}{20}$	$\frac{14}{20}$	$\frac{20}{20}$	$\frac{19}{20}$
Companion Dogs	$\frac{20}{20}$	$\frac{11}{20}$	$\frac{18}{20}$	$\frac{18}{20}$	$\frac{16}{20}$

5 What percentage did the companion dogs score overall?

   a 58%   b 63%   c 72%   **d 83%**   e 90%

6 What fraction of the highest possible score was given for obedience?

   a $\frac{1}{2}$ b $\frac{1}{4}$ c $\frac{1}{5}$ d $\frac{1}{10}$ e $\frac{1}{20}$

7 What was the mean score for the terriers?

   a 15   **b 16**   c 17   d 18   e 19

8 Which **TWO** show categories share the same total score? Underline **TWO** answers.

   a Looks   b Behaviour   c Agility   d Obedience   **e Gait**

Class 6 completed a morning weather chart for the school month. Use the chart to answer the questions. Underline one answer for each question.

KEY		DAY	WEEK 1	WEEK 2	WEEK 3	WEEK 4
Sun	☀	Monday	Sun	Cloud	Rain	Cloud
Cloud	☁	Tuesday	Cloud	Rain	Sun	Cloud
Rain	🌧	Wednesday	Cloud	Storm	Cloud	Sun
Storm	⚡	Thursday	Cloud	Rain	Rain	Cloud
		Friday	Sun	Cloud	Sun	Rain

9 Which school week had equal amounts of rain and sunshine?

   a Week 1   b Week 2   **c Week 3**   d Week 4

10 What fraction of the school month had cloud?

   a $\frac{9}{20}$ b $\frac{1}{2}$ c $\frac{4}{5}$ d $\frac{3}{4}$ e $\frac{9}{10}$

11 What percentage of the school month had stormy weather?

   a 0.5%   b 2%   **c 5%**   d 10%   e 20%

12 Which weekday had equal amounts of cloud and rain?

   a Monday   b Tuesday   c Wednesday   **d Thursday**   e Friday

Test 15: Mixed

Which pattern on the right completes the second pair in the same way as the first pair? Underline the correct answer.

1 is to as is to

a b c d e

Which shape on the right is a 3D rotation of the shape on the left? Underline the correct answer.

2

a b c d e

Which pattern completes the grid? Underline the correct answer.

3

a b c d e

Complete these sequences.

4   −320   −200   −80   40   160   _____   _____

5   $\frac{7}{8}$ $\frac{3}{4}$ $\frac{5}{8}$ $\frac{1}{2}$ $\frac{3}{8}$ _____   _____

6   $73\frac{1}{2}$ _____ $52\frac{9}{10}$ _____ $32\frac{3}{10}$ 22 $11\frac{7}{10}$

7   _____   6.00606   _____   600.606   6006.06   60060.6   600606

The train to Port Sunlight leaves Moorfields at 11:35. The journey takes 17 minutes, but the train is delayed by 11 minutes. Tickets for the journey are £3.35 each way.

8 What time does the train arrive in Port Sunlight? _____

9 How much does it cost for a return journey? _____

10 Mrs Cohen buys four single tickets with a £20 note. How much change does she receive? _____

Erica rolled two dice and made a note of all the potential scores in a grid. If she scored 1 on both dice she would score 2 and if she scored 6 on both dice, she would score 12. Answer the following questions as fractions in their simplest form.

	1	2	3	4	5	6
1	2	3	4	5	6	7
2	3	4	5	6	7	8
3	4	5	6	7	8	9
4	5	6	7	8	9	10
5	6	7	8	9	10	11
6	7	8	9	10	11	12

11 What is the probability that Erica scores a 6? _____

12 What is the probability that Erica scores an even number? _____

Time for a break! ★ Go to Puzzle Page 74 →

Total

Test 16: Sequences

Continue these sequences.

1. 9513   8402   7291   6180   5069   _____   _____

2. 1551   1331   1111   891   671   _____   _____

3. −82   −60   −38   −16   6   _____   _____

Complete these sequences.

4. $\frac{1}{8}$ $\frac{1}{2}$ _____ $1\frac{1}{4}$ _____   2 $2\frac{3}{8}$

5. $\frac{11}{12}$ $\frac{5}{6}$ $\frac{3}{4}$ $\frac{2}{3}$ _____ $\frac{1}{2}$ _____

6. $1\frac{2}{5}$ _____   1   _____ $\frac{3}{5}$ $\frac{2}{5}$ $\frac{1}{5}$

Continue these sequences.

7. 0.003   0.03   0.3   3   30   _____   _____

8. −900   −650   −400   −150   100   _____   _____

9. 1.92   4.28   6.64   9   11.36   _____   _____

Complete these sequences.

10. 3125   625   _____   _____   5   1   0.2

11. 1440   _____   48   12   4   2   _____

12. _____   48   _____   192   384   768   1536

Test 17: Word Problems

Test time: 0 — 5 — 10 minutes

Mr Khan is planning a new garden. He designs a pond, surrounded by a patio, a lawn and a flower bed. Use the plan to answer the following questions. Underline the correct answer for each question.

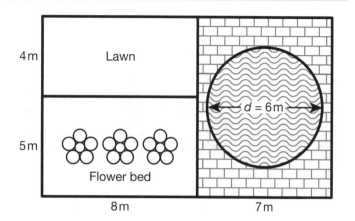

1 What is the radius of the pond?

a 12 m   b 8 m   c 3 cm   d 6 m   e 3 m

2 What is the area of the lawn and flower bed?

a 20 m²   b 32 m²   c 40 m²   d 72 m²   e 135 m²

3 What fraction of the whole garden is the area of the flower bed?

a $\frac{1}{4}$ b $\frac{8}{27}$ c $\frac{1}{3}$ d $\frac{9}{135}$ e $\frac{40}{67}$

4 What is the perimeter of the lawn as a fraction of the perimeter of the whole garden?

a $\frac{1}{6}$ b $\frac{1}{4}$ c $\frac{1}{3}$ d $\frac{1}{2}$ e $\frac{3}{4}$

Mrs Khan buys 24 rose bushes at £3.99 each, 145 flowering bulbs at £1.28 each and 20 shrubs at £7.99 each. Underline one answer for each question.

5 How much do the flowering bulbs cost?

a £125.60   b £130.72   c £184.60   d £185.60   e £578.55

6 How much do the shrubs cost?

a £149.80   b £159.08   c £159.80   d £169.08   e £169.80

7 Mrs Khan hands over £500. How much change does she receive?

a £58.84   b £63.55   c £62.85   d £68.84   e £68.94

Test 18: **Non-verbal Reasoning**

Test time: 0 — 5 — 10 minutes

Which pattern on the right completes the second pair in the same way as the first pair? Underline the correct answer.

1. is to as is to …

   a   b   c   d   e

2. is to as is to

   a   b   c   d   e

3. is to as is to

   a   b   c   d   e

4. is to as  is to

   a   b   c   d   e

Which shape on the right is a 3D rotation of the shape on the left? Underline the correct answer.

Example:

a   b   <u>c</u>   d   e

5.

   a   b   c   d   e

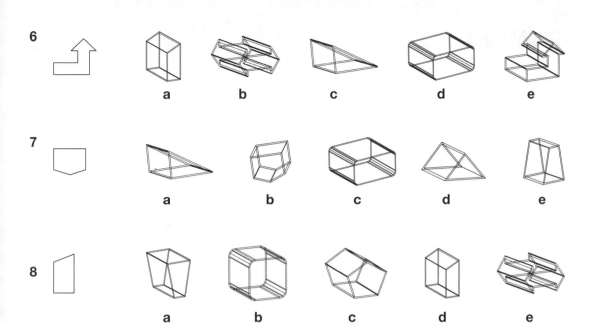

There is a set of pictures on the left with a missing picture shown by a question mark. Underline the correct option from the right to complete the set.

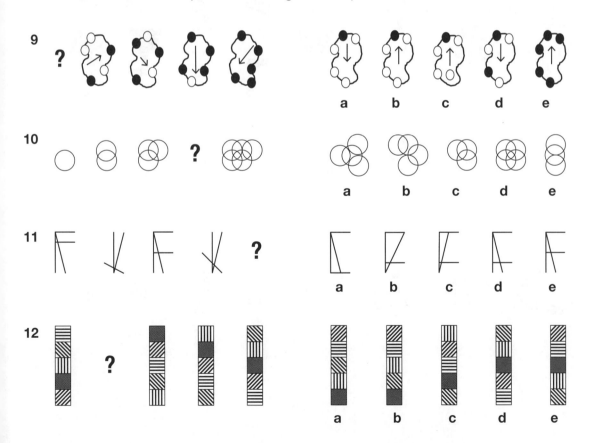

Test 19: **Mixed**

Test time: 0 — 5 — 10 minutes

Complete these sequences.

1   6720   5150   _____   2010   _____   −1130   −2700

2   8   27   64   125   216   _____   _____

3   30 $28\frac{1}{4}$ _____ $24\frac{3}{4}$ 23   _____ $19\frac{1}{2}$

4   3   9   _____   81   _____   729   2187

Which pattern on the right completes the second pair in the same way as the first pair? Underline the correct answer.

5  is to as 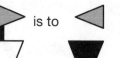 is to
   a   b   c   d   e

6 is to as is to
   a   b   c   d   e

7 is to as is to
   a   b   c   d   e

Mrs Hou owns the New Peking restaurant which has this lunchtime menu. Use it to answer the following questions.

Any meat, chicken, fish or vegetable dish with the following sauce:			
Chow Mein	£4.85	Szechuan	£4.60
Sweet and Sour	£4.80	Satay	£4.65
Peking	£4.55	Sides	
Black Bean	£4.60	Fried Rice	£1.75
Yellow Bean	£4.45	Boiled Rice	£1.00
Oyster Sauce	£4.50	Chips	£1.50
Curry	£4.40	Prawn crackers	No charge

8 Mr Hodge orders one vegetables in yellow bean sauce with fried rice, one chicken curry with boiled rice and one beef in black bean sauce with chips.

What is the total cost for Mr Hodge? _____ [1]

9 Danny orders sweet and sour pork and vegetables in oyster sauce for his friend. They share one portion of fried rice.

How much change does Danny receive from £20? _____ [2]

10 Mrs Tan is having a party so she orders two sweet and sour cod, both with boiled rice, three chicken in Szechuan sauce, each with chips, and three vegetable satays with three portions of fried rice. She goes home and divides the food between 18 people.

How much does the total bill come to? _____ [3]

11 Phil orders chicken chow mein and vegetables in satay sauce with a portion of fried rice and a portion of chips. He pays with one £10 pound note and one £5 pound note. His change is made up from the smallest number of coins possible.

What coins does he receive? _____ [3]

Total [20]

Test 20: **Data**

This chart shows the conversion between British pounds and US dollars. Use the chart to answer the following questions. Underline the correct answer.

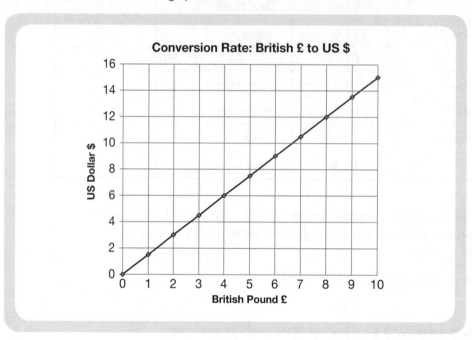

1. How many US dollars can I get for £4?

   a $3   b $4   c $5   d $6   e $7

2. How many British pounds can I get for $12?

   a £6   b £7   c £8   d £9   e £10

3. Estimate how many US dollars I could get for £20.

   a $22   b $24   c $26   d $28   e $30

4. Estimate how many British pounds I could get for $240.

   a £100   b £120   c £140   d £160   e £180

This Venn diagram is used to sort data. Look at the diagram and use it to work out where to place the numbers below. Underline the correct answer.

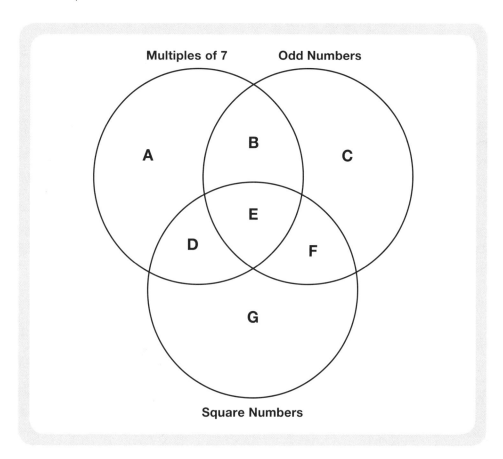

Where do the following numbers fit?

5   49   A   B   C   D   E   F   G

6   25   A   B   C   D   E   F   G

7   98   A   B   C   D   E   F   G

8   225   A   B   C   D   E   F   G

9   84   A   B   C   D   E   F   G

Test 21: Word Problems

1 Chrissy buys some wild-bird food for £7.85 and some squirrel food for £9.24 at the pet shop. What is the total cost of her shopping? Underline the correct answer.

　a £16.09　**b** £16.19　**c** £17.09　**d** £17.19　**e** £17.90

2 Caleb buys a £60 desk that has been reduced by 16%. How much does Caleb pay for the desk? Underline the correct answer.

　a £6.00　**b** £9.60　**c** £50.40　**d** £51.00　**e** £54.00

3 Polly downloads six apps costing between £2.75 and £8. There is a special offer of five apps for £5. What is the greatest saving Polly can make? Underline the correct answer.

　a £30.00　**b** £35.00　**c** £40.00　**d** £43.00　**e** £48.00

4 Pabiur buys a car for £8460 and agrees to pay regular equal payments over 18 months. How much does he pay each month? Underline the correct answer.

　a £403　**b** £450　**c** £467　**d** £470　**e** £480

5 Nick goes to a book shop and buys two calendars for £9.99 each and three diaries for £4.78 each. Nick pays with two £20 notes. How much change does he get? Underline the correct answer.

　a £5.68　**b** £5.77　**c** £15.68　**d** £34.23　**e** £34.32

6 Dot makes 12 jars of jam. She makes 3.24 kg of jam which just fills each jar. Once they are all filled, Dot weighs the 12 jars of jam and they weigh 4.872 kg. How heavy was each jar before it was filled? Underline the correct answer.

　a 0.136 g　**b** 1.36 g　**c** 13.6 g　**d** 136 g　**e** 1360 g

7 Eight large cakes require 9.6 kg of batter. How much batter is required to make five large cakes? Underline the correct answer.

　a 1.2 kg　**b** 1.92 kg　**c** 6 kg　**d** 15.36 kg　**e** 48 kg

Test 22: Word Problems

Test time: 0   5   10 minutes

The whole school is going on a trip to the zoo. There are 632 pupils and 32 teachers. Tickets to the zoo cost £24.80 for an adult and there is 50% off for children. The cost of coach hire is £310 for the day and there are 53 seats on a coach.

1 What is the total cost for ticket prices into the zoo? _____ [3]

2 What is the total cost for coaches so that everyone can get to the zoo? _____ [2]

3 What is the cost per child for a ticket and coach travel? _____ [2]

4 What is the cost per teacher for a ticket and coach travel? _____ [2]

Mo has a new rectangular dog basket which has an area of 9600 cm^2 and is 120 cm long. The old rectangular dog basket had an area of 7200 cm^2 and was 80 cm long.

5 What is the difference in the width between the old and the new dog basket? _____ [3]

6 What is the difference in the perimeter between the old and new dog basket? _____ [2]

7 Rose has some 1 cm cubes. She has a box with sides 12 cm × 4 cm × 5 cm. How many of the cubes will fit into the box? _____ [1]

8 Inside each 1 cm cube, Rose has placed five beads. How many beads will there be in the box? _____ [1]

9 Rose places ten boxes into a crate and five crates on the shelf. How many beads are there in total on the shelf? _____ [1]

Total [17]

Test 23: **Non-verbal Reasoning**

Test time: 0 — 5 — 10 minutes

Which shape on the right is a 3D rotation of the shape on the left? Underline the correct answer.

Example:

                a   b   <u>c</u>   d   e

1

                a   b   c   d   e

2

                a   b   c   d   e

3

                a   b   c   d   e

4

                a   b   c   d   e

5

                a   b   c   d   e

Test continues after Answers section →

Answers

Test 1: Non-verbal Reasoning

1. **c** (shaded squares and black triangles follow diagonal lines)
2. **d** (vertical and horizontal symmetry)
3. **e** (rotational symmetry)
4. **b** (diagonal symmetry)
5. **d** (arrow rotates 45° clockwise)
6. **e** (horizontal line moves downwards; lines increase by 1)
7. **b** (black and white squares decrease and alternate; arrows rotate 90° anticlockwise)
8. **e** (number of internal shapes increases; triangle colour alternates)
9. **a** (sides on outer shape decrease by 1, colour alternates; sides on middle shape increase by 1, shading alternates vertical/horizontal; inner circle colour alternates)
10. **d** (vertical and horizontal lines on opposite faces so cannot touch)
11. **e** (two dots must be other way round when four dots on top face)
12. **b** (right-hand face of net must rotate as face drops downwards)
13. **d** (white trapeziums on opposite faces so cannot touch)

Test 2: Data

1. 80 ((80 + 60 + 85 + 95) ÷ 4)
2. 40 (95 − 55)
3. 75 (order the numbers and work out middle value)
4. 50
5. 14:25
6. 38 min
7. 11:58
8. 10 min
9. 10 teaspoons
10. Pick & Mix Salad
11. 698
12. 58% $\frac{2.9}{5} = \frac{29}{50} = \frac{58}{100}$

Test 3: Word Problems

1. £68.95, i.e. Ozzy's Offers (£9.85 × 7 as there are 3 free)
2. £142 (£3.99 − £1.15 = £2.84; £2.84 × 50 = £142)
3. 3 h (15 ÷ 5 per hour)
4. 13 (6 + 8 + 4 + 5 = 23; 23 × £3.50 = £80.50; £1000 ÷ £80.50 = 12.42, so 13 hours)
5. 83 (500 ÷ 6)
6. 33 (500 ÷ 3 = 166 gives every 3rd; 166 ÷ 5 = 33 gives every 5th of these)

Test 4: Word Problems

1. 300 (10 × 6 × 5 = 300, so the box is 300 cm³; 1 × 1 × 1 = 1 cm³; 300 ÷ 1 = 300 cubes)
2. 900 (300 cubes × 3 beads)
3. £72 (8p × 900 beads)
4. 133 (12 + 11² = 133)
5. 2653 (52 + 51² = 2653)
6. Pattern 12 (13 + 12² = 157)
7. 35p (£40 − £8.15 = £31.85. Balloons: 140 × 4p = £5.60. £31.85 − £5.60 = £26.25. Glow sticks: 25 × 3 boxes = 75. £26.25 ÷ 75 = 35p)
8. £9.27 (10% discount = £5.60 ÷ 10 = 56p. 20% discount = 56p × 2 = £1.12 £8.15 change + £1.12 = £9.27)
9. 5 (75 ÷ 15)

Test 5: Mixed

1. **e** (in each row, colours follow in order)
2. **a** (in each row, patterns follow in order but colours alternate)
3. **d** (each quarter is rotated anticlockwise)
4. **a** ((30 + 15 + 25 + 30) ÷ 4)
5. **a** (Cricket) and **c** (Rugby)
6. **d** (30 is the most common score)
7. **c** (3 × £1.19 + 3 × 0.75 + £3.75 + £2.69 + £4.25 = £16.51; £20 − £16.51 = £3.49)
8. **c** (2 × £2.50 + 2 × 0.75 = £6.50; £6.50 ÷ 100 × 80 = £5.20)
9. **e** (12 × 50 × 30 × 2)
10. **b** (80 − 56)
11. **a** (80 − 24 − 38)
12. **c** (80 − 42)

Test 6: Non-verbal Reasoning

1. **d** (shape rotates clockwise, shading darkens; internal shapes do not rotate but colour alternates)
2. **a** (cross-hatched square rolls clockwise round outside of other two squares whose colour alternates)
3. **e** (number of angles increases by one)

4 e (sides on outer shape decrease by 1; star colour alternates)
5 e (two black hearts on opposite faces so cannot touch)
6 b (arrow always points to/from black face)
7 d (with cross-hatched front face and diagonal lines on side face, top must have lines from left to right, not vertical)
8 e (with top face white and front face vertical lines, side face must be a cross)
9 a (grid is symmetrical)
10 d (in each row, patterns follow in order)
11 e (colours alternate and shapes decrease in size)
12 e (in each row, patterns follow in order but colours alternate)

Test 7: Data

1–2 10% of 480 = 48

1 96 (20% is 2 × 48)
2 192 (40% is 4 × 48)
3 Cartoons (40%) and Comedy (10%)
4 C (20 is in 4 and 5 × tables)
5 D (60 is in 4, 5 and 6 × tables)
6 B (96 is in 4 and 6 × tables)
7 F (110 is in 5 × table)
8 2012   9 2016
10 2007   11 545

Test 8: Word Problems

1 d (40 ÷ 4 = 10 white; 40 ÷ 10 × 3 = 12 yellow; 40 − 10 − 12 = 18 blue)
2 d $\left(10 + 12 = 22; \frac{22}{40} = 55\%\right)$
3 c $\left(12 + 18 = \frac{30}{40} = \frac{3}{4}\right)$
4 e (22 cm × 30 cm × 25 cm)
5 c (22 cm × 30 cm × 2 + 30 cm × 25 cm × 2 + 22 cm × 25 cm × 2)
6 d (£8.00 ÷ 5)
7 b (every 1 cm on the map is 500 000 cm in real distance; 500 000 cm is the same as 5 km; 30 km ÷ 5 km is 6 cm on the map)
8 c (60 min ÷ 65 km = 0.923 min; 0.923 min × 30 km = 27.69 min. Round up to 28 min)

Test 9: Word Problems

1 $\frac{1}{4}$ of a pizza (common denominator is 12 so fractions become Ravi = $\frac{8}{12}$; Charlie = $\frac{9}{12}$; Nadia = $\frac{6}{12}$; Selina = $\frac{10}{12}$. Add up the fractions = $\frac{33}{12}$ slices of pizza which is 2 whole pizzas and $\frac{9}{12}$ so Beth ate $\frac{3}{12}$ or $\frac{1}{4}$ of a pizza.)
2 Selina $\left(\frac{10}{12}\text{ of a pizza}\right)$
3 Beth $\left(\frac{3}{12}\text{ of a pizza}\right)$
4 24 (120 books ÷ 2 = 60 paperback books; 10% is 60 ÷ 10 = 6; 40% is 4 × 6 = 24)
5 9 (120 books ÷ 2 = 60 hardback books; 10% is 60 ÷ 10 = 6; 60% is 6 × 6 = 36 hardback fiction books. 36 ÷ 4 = 9 so 9 by his favourite author)
6 27 (Although this question is about paperback and not hardback books, there is an equal number of both. If 9 out of 36 are by his favourite author, then 27 are fiction not by his favourite author.)
7 £1983.90 (£389 ÷ 10 = £38.90 which is 10%. £38.90 × 3 = £116.70 which is the 30% profit. £116.70 × 17 televisions = £1983.90 total profit made online.)
8 £661.30 (£389 ÷ 10 = £38.90 which is 10%. £38.90 × 17 televisions = £661.30. This is the additional 10% profit he would make compared to selling online.)

Test 10: Mixed

1 56 (280 ÷ 10 × 2 = 56)
2 14 (280 ÷ 10 ÷ 2 = 14)
3 $\frac{7}{20}$ $\left(25\% + 10\% = 35\%\ \frac{35}{100} = \frac{7}{20}\right)$
4 112 (280 ÷ 10 × 4 = 112)
5 d (90° clockwise rotation)
6 a (flag black, grey, white; arrow short, medium, long; flag/arrow swap top/bottom)
7 e (diagonal lines on opposite faces so cannot touch)
8 d (diagonal arrows on opposite faces so cannot touch)
9 $\frac{19}{20}$ $\left(12 \times 10 = 120\text{ slices}; 6\text{ slices eaten}; 114\text{ left.} = \frac{6}{120} = \frac{1}{20}\text{ so }\frac{19}{20}\text{ left}\right)$
10 $\frac{11}{12}$ $\left(114 - 4 = 110\text{ left}\ \frac{110}{120} = \frac{11}{12}\right)$
11 60% $\left(110 - 38 = 72\text{ left}\ \frac{72}{120} = \frac{6}{10} = 60\%\right)$

12 $\frac{2}{5}$ $\left(40\% = \frac{4}{10} = \frac{2}{5}\right)$

Test 11: Non-verbal Reasoning

1 c (outline of shape changes from solid to short dashes)
2 c (number of arrows matches number of sides)
3 d (patterns swap over and shape is rotated 90° anticlockwise)
4 e (matching shape is 3D)
5 a (ovals become circles with patterns distributed anticlockwise, starting with top pattern in left-hand oval)
6 c   7 a   8 d   9 b
10 a (rotational symmetry)
11 c (dots and squares form diagonals; pennant and rhombus complete grid so only one in each row/column)
12 c (moon shape rotates clockwise)
13 e (diagonal symmetry)

Test 12: Sequences

1 1969, 2116 (+ 147)
2 8868, 8739 (− 129)
3 −4250, −4200 (+ 50)
4 $\frac{1}{2}, 1 \left(+ \frac{1}{6}\right)$
5 $\frac{8}{9}, \frac{5}{9} \left(- \frac{1}{9}\right)$
6 $5\frac{1}{4}, 9 \left(+ 1\frac{1}{4}\right)$
7 0.02147, 0.002147 (÷ 10)
8 0.43, 0.55 (+ 0.12)
9 2.72, 0.73 (− 1.99)
10 9, 81 (× 3)
11 8064, 504 (÷ 2)
12 6, 36 (× 1, × 2, × 3, × 4, × 5, × 6)

Test 13: Word Problems

1–3 There are four times as many women as men so there is one man for every four women. 1 + 4 = 5 so out of 640 people, 640 ÷ 5 = 128 are men; 512 are women. There are seven times more non-managers than managers so for every manager, there are seven non-managers. 1 + 7 = 8 so out of 640 people, 80 are managers and 560 are non-managers. One in eight didn't go to university. 640 ÷ 8 = 80 people who did not go to university so 560 did go to university.

1 560
2 16 (80 people who did not go to university. 80 ÷ 5 = 16 men.)
3 56 (512 women ÷ 8 × 7 people who went to university = 448. 448 ÷ 8 = 56 managers)

4–6 Kishor = 6 per hour, Bharani = 4 per hour, Gnanan = 3 per hour, Thanikai = 6 per hour.

4 3
5 Kishor and Thanikai
6 57 (6 + 4 + 3 + 6 = 19 per hour; 19 per hour × 3 hours = 57)

7–10 4 cleaners × 2 h = 8 h (480 min) of cleaning. If there are 20 rooms, 480 min ÷ 20 = 24 min per room.

7 24 min (or 0.4 h)
8 4 h (half the number of cleaners will take twice as long)
9 1 h 20 min (480 min ÷ 6 = 80 min)
10 10 cleaners (480 min ÷ 48 min)

Test 14: Data

1 c   2 a
3 c   4 b
5 d $\left(20 + 11 + 18 + 18 = 83 \quad \frac{83}{100} = 83\%\right)$
6 c $\left(20 \text{ out of } 100 = \frac{1}{5}\right)$
7 b (18 + 13 + 15 + 15 + 19 = 80; 80 ÷ 5 categories = 16)
8 a and e   9 c
10 a (9 out of 20)
11 c $\left(\text{storm} = \frac{1}{20} = 5\%\right)$ 12 d

Test 15: Mixed

1 c (number of balls equals number of sides)
2 b
3 e (rows 1 and 4, shape rotated 90° clockwise; rows 2 and 3, 90° anticlockwise)
4 280, 400 (+ 120)
5 $\frac{1}{4}, \frac{1}{8} \left(- \frac{1}{8}\right)$
6 $63\frac{1}{5}, 42\frac{3}{5} \left(-10\frac{3}{10}\right)$
7 0.600606, 60.0606 (× 10)
8 12:03 (11:35 + 17 min + 11 min)
9 £6.70 (£3.35 × 2)
10 £6.60   11 $\frac{5}{36}$
12 $\frac{1}{2} \left(\frac{18}{36} \text{ in its simplest form}\right)$

Test 16: Sequences

1 3958, 2847 (− 1111)
2 451, 231 (− 220)
3 28, 50 (+ 22)
4 $\frac{7}{8}, 1\frac{5}{8} \left(+ \frac{3}{8}\right)$
5 $\frac{7}{12}, \frac{5}{12} \left(- \frac{1}{12}\right)$

6 $1\frac{1}{5}, \frac{4}{5} \left(-\frac{1}{5}\right)$
7 300, 3000 (× 10)
8 350, 600 (+ 250)
9 13.72, 16.08 (+ 2.36)
10 125, 25 (÷ 5)
11 240, 2 (÷ 6, ÷ 5, ÷ 4, ÷ 3, ÷ 2, ÷ 1)
12 24, 96 (× 2)

Test 17: Word Problems

1 e (radius = $\frac{1}{2}$ diameter, d; d = 6m so radius = 3m)
2 d (width of lawn and flower bed = 4m + 5m = 9m; area of lawn and flower bed = 9m × 8m = 72m²)
3 b (area whole garden = 9m × 15m = 135m²; area flower bed = 5m × 8m = 40m²; $\frac{40}{135} = \frac{8}{27}$)
4 d (perimeter of lawn = 8m + 4m + 8m + 4m = 24m; perimeter whole garden = 15m + 9m + 15m + 9m = 48m; $\frac{24}{48} = \frac{1}{2}$)
5 d (145 × £1.28)
6 c (20 × £7.99)
7 a

Test 18: Non-verbal Reasoning

1 a (colour changed and shapes placed in straight line)
2 b (number of shapes equals number of sides, with shapes overlapped)
3 a (shape rotated 90° clockwise; then is a reflection of the other shape)
4 d (shape rotated 180°; number of new shapes equals number of sides)
5 a   6 e   7 b   8 d
9 b (one ball changes from white to black while the arrow rotates clockwise)
10 d (one circle added to existing pattern)
11 d (V shape alternates; when V points upwards there are two horizontal lines; lower line moves downwards)
12 a (pattern on blocks moves down by one)

Test 19: Mixed

1 3580, 440 (− 1570)
2 343, 512 (cube numbers)
3 $26\frac{1}{2}, 21\frac{1}{4} \left(-1\frac{3}{4}\right)$
4 27, 243 (× 3)
5 a (upper shape reflected; black shape rotated and moved to bottom; lower two shapes swap colour)
6 e (whole shape rotates 90° clockwise; outer shape moves to middle and other shapes increase in size)
7 e (same number of sides as arrows, with cross-hatched pattern)
8 £17.70 (£4.45 + £1.75 + £4.40 + £1.00 + £4.60 + £1.50)
9 £8.95 (total cost = £11.05; £20 − £11.05 = £8.95)
10 £49.10 ((2 × £4.80) + (2 × £1.00) + (3 × £4.60) + (3 × £1.50) + (3 × £4.65) + (3 × £1.75))
11 £2, 20p, 5p (£4.85 + £4.65 + £1.75 + £1.50 = £12.75; change = £15.00 − £12.75 = £2.25)

Test 20: Data

1 d $6   2 c £8
3 e $30 ($15 × 2)
4 d £160 ($12 = £8 so 20 × £8)
5 E (multiple of 7, odd and square)
6 F (odd and square)
7 A (multiple of 7)
8 F (odd and square)
9 A (multiple of 7)

Test 21: Word Problems

1 c £17.09 (£7.85 + £9.24)
2 c £50.40 (£60 × 0.84)
3 b £35.00 (5 apps @ £8 each = £40; £40 − £5 for 5 apps = £35)
4 d £470 $\left(\frac{£8460}{18}\right)$
5 a £5.68 (2 × £20 − (£9.99 × 2) − (£4.78 × 3))
6 d 136 g $\left(\frac{4.872\text{kg} - 3.24\text{kg}}{12}\right)$
7 c 6 kg $\left(\frac{9.6\text{kg}}{8} \times 5\right)$

Test 22: Word Problems

1 £8630.40 (32 × £24.80 = £793.60; £24.80 ÷ 2 = £12.40 for a child's ticket; £12.40 × 632 = £7836.80; total cost of tickets = £793.60 + £7836.80 = £8630.40)
2 £4030 (632 pupils + 32 teachers = 664 people; each coach has 53 seats: 664 ÷ 53 = 12.5 so 13 coaches needed; £310 × 13 coaches = £4030)
3 £18.47 (£4030 ÷ 664 people = £6.07 each; child's ticket plus coach fare = £12.40 + £6.07 = £18.47)
4 £30.87 (teacher's ticket plus coach fare = £24.80 + £6.07 = £30.87)
5 10 cm (old basket: area ÷ length = width = 7200 cm ÷ 80 cm = 90 cm; new basket : width = 9600 cm ÷ 120 cm =

80 cm; difference = 90 cm − 80 cm = 10 cm)

6 60 cm (old basket perimeter = 80 cm + 90 cm + 80 cm + 90 cm = 340 cm; new basket perimeter = 120 cm + 80 cm + 120 cm + 80 cm = 400 cm; difference = 400 cm − 340 cm = 60 cm)

7 240 (in box: 12 × 1 cm cubes fit in 12 cm; 4 × 1 cm cubes fit in 4 cm and 5 × 1 cm cubes fit in 5 cm. 12 × 4 × 5 = 240 cubes)

8 1200 (240 × 5)

9 60 000 (1200 beads × 10 boxes × 5 crates)

Test 23: Non-verbal Reasoning

1 a   **2** a   **3** d
4 d   **5** b
6 a (number of balls equals number of points; line of balls points to top right; first ball at bottom same colour as upper shape, e.g. white triangle = 1st ball white)
7 c (shape rotates 90° so lines change direction; centre section changes colour)
8 d (number of triangles equals number of arrows; shading changes to opposite so vertical becomes horizontal)
9 a (shapes join at base and the lines rotate approximately 180°)

Test 24: Mixed

1 b 18 $\left(\frac{10+17+20+25}{4}\right)$

2 b Toys 2 (Toys 1: 32 − 5 = 27, Toys 2: 35 − 3 = 32, Toys 3: 20 − 10 = 10, Toys 4: 25 − 10 = 15, Toys 5: 25 − 20 = 5)

3 d 40% $\left(\frac{32}{32+3+15+10+20}\times 100\right)$

4 e 92.75 km $\left(\frac{53\,\text{km}}{20}\times 35\right)$

5 c 240 ((4 × 3) × (4 × 5))

6 e   **7** b   **8** d

9 b (£349 × 5 people = £1745; £480 × 5 people = £2400; difference in price = £2400 − £1745 = £655)

10 d (2 adults + $\frac{1}{2}$ adult + 2 × $\frac{3}{4}$ adult means they pay 4 × adult price = 4 × £480 = £1920 per week, so for two weeks £1920 × 2 = £3840)

11 e (£1745 + £3840 = £5585)

12 b (£2400 + £3840 = £6240; half of bill = £6240 ÷ 2 = £3120)

Test 25: Data

1, 2 & 4 10% of 420 = 42; 5% = 21

1 105 $\left(\frac{420}{100}\times 25\right)$

2 Viking (Viking 40%, Tudor 20%)

3 147 (35%: 3 × 42 + 21)

4 63 (15%: 42 + 21)

5 17 $\left(\frac{17+15+20+14+19}{5}\right)$

6 5 (19 − 14)

7 19 (median is middle value: 14, 16, 19, 20, 20)

8 6 (highest score = 19; lowest score = 13; 19 − 13 = 6)

9 Planet1 (Planet1 has a 13.0 MP camera, 64 GB storage and 8 GB RAM)

10 £46 (£125 + £279 = £404; £450 − £404 = £46)

11 Pro Pad (20 games, a camera and under £100)

12 £1040 (Pix32 has five stars; 8 @ £130 = £1040)

Test 26: Word Problems

1 a 9 (54 ÷ 6)
   b 18 (9 × 2)
   c 27 (9 × 3)

2 $\frac{11}{120}\left(1-\left(\frac{40}{120}+\frac{24}{120}+\frac{45}{120}\right)\right)$

3 15% (24 − 20.4 = 3.6; $\frac{3.6}{24}=\frac{3}{20}=15\%$)

4 a–d (If they all have an equal number now, 144 ÷ 4 = 36 cards each. 36 is $\frac{2}{3}$ of what Jake started with so he had 36 + 18 = 54. 36 is $\frac{3}{4}$ of what Jethro started with so he had 36 + 12 = 48. Harry gave Ryan two cards so he started with 36 + 2 = 38 cards. Ryan was given 18 + 12 + 2 = 32 cards so he started with 4. (54 + 48 + 36 + 4 = 144))
   a 54   b 4   c 48   d 38

5 a £47.70 (£14.38 + £3.97 + £29.35)
   b £2.30 ((£20 + £20 + £10) − £47.70)

6 a £3.22 ((2 × 0.35) + (4 × 0.45) + (3 × 0.24))
   b £2.33 ((4 × 0.35) + (1 × 0.45) + (2 × 0.24))

7 15:17 (14:25 + 12 min + 35 min + 5 min)

Test 27: Word Problems

1 e (10 + 20² = 410)
2 d (100 + 200² = 40 100)
3 a (Pattern 5 is 5 + 10² = 105)
4 c (10% = £208 ÷ 10 = £20.80; 35% profit = £20.80 × 3.5 = £72.80; total profit from selling 16 smart

phones online = £72.80 × 16 = £1164.80)

5 a (additional 5% profit compared to selling online = £20.80 × 0.5 = £10.40; £10.40 × 16 smart phones = £166.40)

6 c (£208 × 8 smart phones = £1664 × 35% = £2246.40 and £1664 × 40% = £2329.60. Add together the two amounts: £2246.40 + £2329.60 = £4576. Cost of stock is £208 × 16 = £3328. The total profit is £4576 − £3328 = £1248.)

Test 28: Non-verbal Reasoning

1 b (black shading on opposite faces so cannot touch)

2 d (arrows that go from edge to edge on a face always point towards or away from a face with a diagonal arrow, not across)

3 e (face with black dot is opposite white face so they cannot touch)

4 d (two of the faces shaded white are opposite so cannot touch)

5 a (face with single dot and face with two dots are opposite so cannot touch)

6 e   **7 e**   **8 b**
9 c   **10 d**

Test 29: Mixed

1 a (white shape rotated 90°; black shape moved to middle; grey shape rotated 90°)

2 b (shape rotated 90° clockwise, reduced in size and coloured grey)

3 d (shape rotated 90° clockwise, reflected about vertical axis and coloured white; black version of shape added to fill the rectangle)

4 6144, 1536 (÷ 2)

5 $11\frac{1}{6}, 17$ (+ $1\frac{1}{6}$)

6 0, −1.06 (− 0.53)

7 2187, 27 (÷ 3)

8 23.21, 27.61 (+ 4.4)

9 35 (6 + 9 + 8 + 6 + 3 + 2 + 1)

10 3 people (in 9 homes)

11 12 (6 + 3 + 2 + 1)

12 $\frac{1}{3}$ (12 out of 36)

13 $\frac{1}{4}$ (9 out of 36)

14 15 (36 − 12 − 9)

Test 30: Sequences

1 25, 9 (descending odd squares)

2 21, 34 (Fibonacci sequence: number 1 + number 2 = number 3 and so on)

3 −729, −2187 (× 3)

4 0 and −91 (− 91)

5 11, 19 (prime numbers)

6 −91, −112 (− 7)

7 0.001, 64 000 (× 20)

8 17 and 20.81 (+1.27)

9 $1\frac{1}{8}, 1\frac{3}{8}$ (+ $\frac{1}{4}$)

10 0.925, 0.4625 (÷ 2)

11 $3\frac{7}{9}$ and $6\frac{4}{9}$ (+ $\frac{8}{9}$)

12 14 and −2.24 (− 2.32)

Test 31: Data

1 25 min (16:17 − 15:52)

2 15:10 (Leave Bridgnorth 12:20, arrive at Hampton Loade 12:37, leave Hampton Loade 14:22, arrive Kidderminster 15:10)

3 13:31 (Leave Bridgnorth 10:25, arrive Bewdley 11:18, leave Bewdley 13:20, arrive Kidderminster 13:31)

4 £44.80 (£12.80 × 2 + £6.40 × 3)

5 £380 (45 × 5 × £12.80 = £2880; £2880 − £2500 = £380)

Test 32: Word Problems

1 e 210 g $\left(\frac{1}{2} \times \frac{1}{3}\right)$ of 1.26 kg

2 d 126 g $\left(\frac{630g - 210g}{100} \times 30\right)$

3 c 2820 cm² ((40 cm × 45 cm) + (6 cm × 40 cm) × 2) + (6 cm × 45 cm) × 2))

4 b 440 (20 × 22)

5 b 20 cm $\left(1 \text{ cm represents } 3.5 \text{ km}, \frac{70}{3.5}\right)$

6 c 14 km (4 × 3.5)

Test 33: Word Problems

1 24p (total cost = £80 − £19.25 change = £60.75; crayons cost 65 × 27p = £17.55; cost of 180 pencils = total cost minus cost of crayons = £60.75 − £17.55 = £43.20; cost of 1 pencil = £43.20 ÷ 180 = 24p)

2 £11.88 (every third pencil is free so he has to buy $\frac{2}{3}$ of 65 (rounded up to a whole pencil); 44 × 27p = £11.88)

3 £55.08 (£11.88 + £43.20)

4–6 Noah has 5 hoodies so 5 × 2 = 10 tops have long sleeves. 1 in 3 tops have long sleeves, so total number of tops = 3 × 10 = 30; $\frac{2}{3}$ of these (20) have short sleeves. Tops are $\frac{1}{4}$ of Noah's clothes, so total number of clothes = 4 × 30 = 120. Of this total, $\frac{3}{4}$ are trousers, so 120 ÷ 4 × 3 = 90. Of this 90, 20% are jeans: 90 ÷ 10 = 9; 9 × 2 = 18)

4 120 total items
5 18 jeans
6 20 short-sleeved tops
7 900 (1st stop: 482 ÷ 2 = 241 passengers get off so 241 + 318 = 559 are on. 2nd stop: 559 + 383 – 42 = 900)
8 1000 (900 ÷ 3 = 300 get off, leaving 600 on; 600 + 400 more = 1000)

Test 34: Mixed

1 30 : 60 : 90 : 120 : 150 (total number of parts = 1 + 2 + 3 + 4 + 5 = 15; smallest share = 450 ÷15)
2 120 ((30 + 60 + 150) ÷ 2)
3 210 (90 + 120)

4–9 In each question, there are two sequences running alternately.

4 9, 50 (odd numbers; + 10)
5 21, 77 (+ 7; – 11)
6 144, 13 (– 12; + 13)
7 30, 120 (+ 15; ÷ 2)
8 63, 68 (+ 17; – 21)
9 140, 5 (÷ 2; + 20)
10 £8.09 (£10 – (97p + 59p + 35p))
11 £1.93 (£1.05 + 39p + 49p)
12 £16.71 (£20 – (£1.55 + £0.30 + £0.39 + £1.05))
13 d   14 b   15 c   16 e

Test 35: Non-verbal Reasoning

1 c (horizontal, vertical and diagonal symmetry)
2 b (vertical and horizontal symmetry)
3 a (diagonal symmetry)
4 d (rotating about centre of grid, each small central square has pattern of three outer squares to its right)
5 d (position of the circles and stars is symmetrical about the diagonal)
6 a (pattern begins with totally black L and upper star, progressing to whiter L and upper star)
7 b (triangle shading alternates vertical/horizontal stripes; rectangle colour repeats black, grey, white)
8 c (pattern of top right L moves to bottom left L)
9 a (pattern in each block moves upwards two places)

Test 36: Data

1 a £3.75 (50% of £2.50 = £1.25; £2.50 + £1.25 = £3.75)
   b £35 (40% of £25 = £10; £25 + £10 = £35)
   c £4.20 (50% of £2.80 = £1.40; £2.80 + £1.40 = £4.20)
2 £38.80 (£6 + 2 × £2.50 + £25 + £2.80)
3 £56.30 (£9.60 + 2 × £3.75 + £35 + £4.20)
4 £27.30 (£12 + £12.50 + £2.80)
5 £42.15 (2 × £9.60 + 5 × £3.75 + £4.20)
6 £32.35 (profit = total retail price – total cost price = (£56.30 + £42.15) – (£38.80 + £27.30))

7–12 100% = 240; 10% = 24; 5% = 12

7 60 (25% is 2 × 24 + 12)
8 96 (40% is 4 × 24)
9 72 (30% is 3 × 24)
10 168 (30% chose Corn Cereal, so 70% did not. 70% is 7 × 24)
11 Porridge (24 children is 10%; and 10% chose Porridge)
12 Bran Cereal (12 children is 5%; 5% chose Bran Cereal)

Test 37: Word Problems

1 b £35.70 (£25 + £3.60 × 2 + £3.50)
2 e £4.30 (£40 – £35.70)
3 d £1.75 (25% of £7)
4 b 333 (1000 cars ÷ 3)
5 c 83 (1000 cars ÷ 12)
6 a 33 (1000 cars ÷ 3 ÷ 10)
7 d 20% (£7.10 ÷ £35.50 × 100)
8 a £35.70 (£51 ÷ 100 × 70%)

Test 38: Word Problems

1 c (42 km ÷ 63 km/h = $\frac{2}{3}$; 60 min ÷ 3 = 20 min. 20 min × 2 = 40 min)
2 e (10:30 a.m. + 40 min + $1\frac{1}{2}$ h + 40 min = 1:20 p.m.)
3 d (total journey = 42 km + 85 km + 62 km = 189 km; 189 ÷ 63 km/h = 3 h; 10 a.m. + 3 h + 30 min + 1 h = 2:30 p.m.)

4–6 Zara plays at 10:00, 10:06, 10:12, ... and all multiples of 6 min up to 11:00. Dora plays the same as Zara plus one additional time between each beat. Melody plays at 10:00, 10:04, 10:08, 10:12, ... and all multiples of 4 min up to 11:00 and Evie plays at 10:00, 10:12, 10:24, 10:36, 10:48, 11:00.

4 e (10:06, 6 is a multiple of 3 and 6)
5 c (10:12, 12 is multiple of 3, 4, 6 and 12)
6 c (all multiples of 12 min, including 10:00 and 11:00 (0, 12, 24, 36, 48, 60))

Test 39: Mixed

1. £1407 (£2100 ÷ 100 × 67)
2. £148.50 (£990 ÷ 100 × 15)
3. 32% (£400 ÷ £1250 × 100)
4. Elle has a biased spinner (1 mark). It lands on 3 more than any other number (1 mark) and more than probability (1 mark).
5. 5 (total score (40) divided by number of spins (8))
6. 250 g (18 cakes need 100 g; 45 cakes is $2\frac{1}{2}$ times 18. $2\frac{1}{2} \times 100\,g = 250\,g$)
7. 11 eggs (If 18 cakes need 3 eggs then 1 egg makes 6 cakes. 66 ÷ 6 = 11)
8. 63 (350 g = $3\frac{1}{2} \times 100\,g$. $18 \times 3\frac{1}{2} = 63$)
9. 270 (1125 g = 15 × 75 g. 18 × 15 = 270)
10. c (+ 0.45)
11. a (+ 1.71)
12. e (× 2)

Test 40: Mixed

1. e (two black faces are opposite so cannot touch)
2. d (faces with cross-hatching and stripes are opposite so cannot touch)
3. e (black and white faces are opposite so cannot touch)
4. e   5. c   6. e
7. a (120 × 38p − £16.80 = £28.80)
8. b (120 ÷ 5 apples = 24; 24 × £1.50 − £16.80 = £19.20)
9. e (10 × 5 apples = 50; 120 − 50 = 70. 10 × £1.50 + 70 × 38p = £41.60; £41.60 − £16.80 = £24.80)
10. e (15 × 14 × 40 × 3)
11. c (25 200 ÷ 2 × 12p)
12. 16.48, 19.15 (+ 0.89)
13. $1\frac{7}{15}, 1\frac{2}{5} \left(-\frac{1}{15}\right)$

Puzzle 1

1 b   2 c   3 a

Puzzle 2

$\frac{2}{3}$	0.667	66.7%
$\frac{4}{50}$	0.08	8%
$\frac{9}{12}$	0.75	75%
$\frac{12}{15}$	0.8	80%
$\frac{7}{14}$	0.5	50%
$\frac{7}{40}$	0.175	17.5%
$\frac{5}{125}$	0.04	4%
$\frac{14}{25}$	0.56	56%

Puzzle 3

×	16	17	18
13	**208**	221	234
14	224	238	**252**
15	240	**255**	270

×	1.4	3.2	2.5
7.2	**10.08**	23.04	18
8.6	12.04	**27.52**	21.5
9.1	12.74	29.12	**22.75**

+	65.29	**31.24**	5.001
0.92	66.21	32.16	5.921
47.692	112.982	78.932	**52.693**
12.21	**77.5**	43.45	17.211

Puzzle 4

A	B	C	D	E	F	G
4	5	6	7	8	9	10
H	I	J	K	L	M	N
11	12	13	14	15	16	17
O	P	Q	R	S	T	U
18	19	20	21	22	23	24
V	W	X	Y	Z		
25	26	1	2	3		

Hidden message: hello have you solved this yet

Puzzle 5

Robot 1: (1, 6)
Robot 2: (11, 8)
Robot 3: (2, 4)

Puzzle 6

Field 1: 16
Field 2: 64
Field 3: 48
Field 4: 64

Puzzle 7

1 36   2 3375   3 21

Puzzle 8

	Places
1	Norwich
2	Manchester
3	Birmingham
4	Gloucester
5	London
6	Liverpool
7	Exeter
8	Chester
9	Durham
10	Leeds
11	York
12	Stafford

Test 23: continued

Which pattern on the right completes the second pair in the same way as the first pair? Underline the correct answer.

6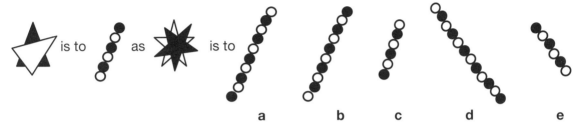

7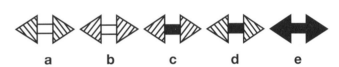

8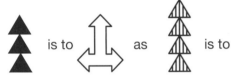

9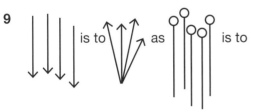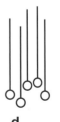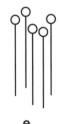

Test 24: Mixed

The children in Year 6 interviewed different year groups in the school to find out which toys were the most popular. They made this table to show their results. Use the table to answer the following questions. Underline the correct answer each time.

		Year 3	Year 4	Year 5	Year 6
Toys 1	Teddies and Dolls	32	25	18	5
Toys 2	Console and Computer Games	3	12	27	35
Toys 3	Jigsaws and Board Games	15	20	12	10
Toys 4	Construction and Craft Toys	10	17	20	25
Toys 5	Outdoor Toys	20	20	25	25

1   What is the mean score for construction and craft toys?

   a 14   **b** 18   **c** 20   **d** 25   **e** 30

2   Which type of toy has the greatest range?

   a Toys 1   **b** Toys 2   **c** Toys 3   **d** Toys 4   **e** Toys 5

3   What percentage of Year 3 children prefer teddies and dolls?

   a 20%   **b** 25%   **c** 32%   **d** 40%   **e** 45%

4   Beth takes 20 minutes to drive the 53 kilometres to work. Ben drives at the same speed but his journey takes 35 minutes. How far does he have to drive to get to work? Underline the correct answer.

   a 60.5 km   **b** 66 km   **c** 70.25 km   **d** 88 km   **e** 92.75 km

5   Demetrius is building a patio 3 metres long by 5 metres wide. He is using square slabs that are 25 centimetres long each side. How many square slabs does he need? Underline the correct answer.

   a 24   **b** 25   **c** 240   **d** 250   **e** 2400

Which shape on the right is a 3D rotation of the shape on the left? Underline the correct answer.

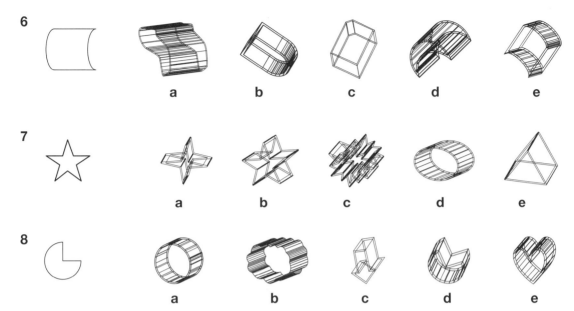

6 a b c d e

7 a b c d e

8 a b c d e

Varna books a family holiday. The cost of flights is £349 per person return from a London airport or £480 per person return from her local airport. The hotel costs £480 per adult per week with a 50% reduction for the youngest child and a 25% reduction for all other children.

9 If Varna, her adult friend and three children book flights, how much would Varna save flying from London compared to her local airport?

a £555   b £655   c £1745   d £2400   e £4145

10 How much would the hotel cost for a two-week stay for Varna, her friend and three children?

a £1440   b £2880   c £3240   d £3840   e £4800

11 Varna plans that they will all go for two weeks and fly from a London airport. How much would this cost?

a £2880   b £3455   c £3650   d £4800   e £5585

12 Varna's friend thinks it would be better to fly from the local airport and she decides to pay half the total bill. How much does Varna now have to pay?

a £2140   b £3120   c £4800   d £5280   e £5880

Test 25: Data

There are 420 pupils at Westfield Primary school. They were each asked which historical period they most enjoyed learning about. Their results are shown on this pie chart. Use it to answer the following questions.

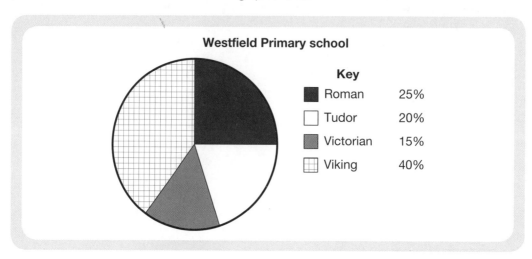

Westfield Primary school

Key:
- Roman 25%
- Tudor 20%
- Victorian 15%
- Viking 40%

1. How many pupils preferred the Roman period? _____

2. Which historical period was twice as popular as another? _____

3. How many pupils preferred either the Tudor or Victorian period? _____

4. How many pupils preferred the Victorian period? _____

The table below shows the scores of five village teams in the Best Village Quiz. They were asked 20 questions in each subject. Use the table to answer the following questions.

	Maths	English	History	Geography	Science
Trysull	17	15	20	14	19
Seisdon	18	16	16	13	17
Swindon	16	17	19	16	18
Heathton	15	15	14	19	19
Wombourne	20	19	20	15	18

5. What was the average score for Trysull? _____

6   What was the range for Heathton? _____

7   What is the median score for history? _____

8   What is the range for geography? _____

The table below shows the latest tablets with their features and costs. Use the table to answer the following questions.

Model	Rating	Storage (GB)	RAM (GB)	Mass (kg)	Camera resolution (MP)	Games	Cost
K1324	*	16	3	0.40	2.0	10	£125
Pix32	*****	64	4	0.51	13.0	50	£130
Planet1	***	64	8	1.76	13.0	35	£279
Pro Tab	*	16	2	0.45	x	10	£95
Tabpad	**	8	2	1.21	x	x	£65
LA 9"	**	8	3	0.85	5.0	x	£120
Pro Pad	***	8	4	0.98	8.0	20	£99

9   Richard wants the highest resolution camera, and storage and RAM are important to him.

Which model is best for Richard? _____

10 Mr Row buys the lightest tablet for his daughter and the tablet with the highest RAM for his son.

How much change will he get from £450? _____

11 Jess wants to play games and take pictures. She has £100 to spend.

Which model is the best for Jess? _____

12 Dan wants to buy eight of the tablets that have the highest rating for his staff.

How much would this cost? _____

Time for a break! ★ *Go to Puzzle Page 76* →

Test 26: **Word Problems**

Test time: 0 — 5 — 10 minutes

1. Morgan, Madison and David share 54 sweets in the ratio 1 : 2 : 3. How many sweets do they each get?

   a Morgan _____   b Madison _____   c David _____

2. Katie buys one extra-large pizza. Katie eats $\frac{1}{3}$ of the pizza. Lily eats $\frac{1}{5}$ of the pizza and Dawn eats $\frac{3}{8}$ of the pizza.

   How much of the pizza is left? _____

3. Summer buys a book in the sale. The original price was £24 and she paid £20.40.

   What percentage of the original price has been taken off? _____

4. Jake, Ryan, Jethro and Harry have 144 playing cards. Jake gives Ryan $\frac{1}{3}$ of his cards, Jethro gives Ryan $\frac{1}{4}$ of his cards and Harry gives Ryan two cards. They now have the same number of cards each. How many cards did they start with?

   a Jake had _____ cards   c Jethro had _____ cards

   b Ryan had _____ cards   d Harry had _____ cards

5. Rani spends £14.38 at the supermarket, £3.97 at the baker's and £29.35 at the butcher's. She hands over two £20 pound notes and one £10 note.

   a How much does she spend in total?   _____

   b How much change does Rani receive? _____

6. If apples (*a*) are 35p each, bananas (*b*) are 45p each and tangerines (*t*) are 24p each, how much is the following?

   a $2a + 4b + 3t =$ _____

   b $4a + 1b + 2t =$ _____

7. The 14:25 bus into town is running 12 minutes late. It takes 35 minutes to arrive in town. My watch is running 5 minutes fast.

   What time does it show on my watch when we reach town? _____

Total 16

50

Test 27: Word Problems

Kayleigh makes a pattern using triangles and squares. She extends the pattern each time and puts the following mathematical equations into her patterns. Underline the correct answer from options **a–e**.

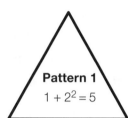

Pattern 1
$1 + 2^2 = 5$

Pattern 2
$2 + 4^2 = 18$

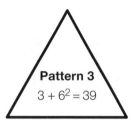

Pattern 3
$3 + 6^2 = 39$

Pattern 4
$4 + 8^2 = 68$

1 What would be the answer for pattern 10?

　a 100　　**b** 110　　**c** 390　　**d** 400　　**e** 410

2 What would be the answer for pattern 100?

　a 41 010　　**b** 40 001　　**c** 40 010　　**d** 40 100　　**e** 41 000

3 Which pattern would give the answer 105?

　a 5　　**b** 6　　**c** 7　　**d** 8　　**e** 9

Henry buys 16 smart phones costing £208 each. When he sells them in his online shop, he adds on 35%. When he sells them in his retail outlet, he adds on 40%.

4 If Henry could sell all of the smart phones online, how much profit would he make? Remember to take off what Henry paid for the smart phones.

　a £20.80　　**b** £72.80　　**c** £1164.80　　**d** £3328　　**e** £4492.80

5 If Henry could sell all of the smart phones in his retail outlet, how much additional profit would he make compared to selling them online?

　a £166.40　　**b** £216.32　　**c** £872.30　　**d** £1664　　**e** £4659.20

6 If Henry sells half of his stock online and the rest in his retail outlet, how much overall profit will he make?

　a £1058　　**b** £1106　　**c** £1248　　**d** £1250　　**e** £1348

Test 28: **Non-verbal Reasoning**

Test time: 0 — 5 — 10 minutes

Which cube cannot be made from the given net? Underline the correct answer.

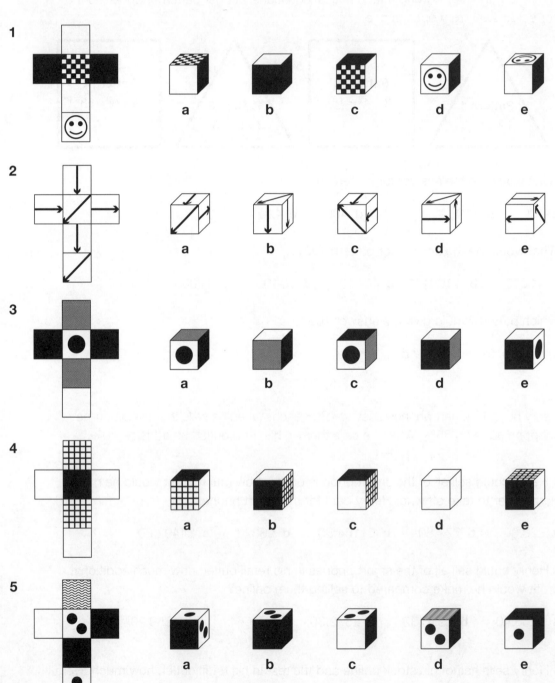

Which shape on the right is a 3D rotation of the shape on the left? Underline the correct answer.

Example:

a   b   <u>c</u>   d   e

6
          a   b   c   d   e

7
          a   b   c   d   e

8
          a   b   c   d   e

9
          a   b   c   d   e

10
          a   b   c   d   e

Test 29: Mixed

Which pattern on the right completes the second pair in the same way as the first pair? Underline the correct answer.

1
    a   b   c   d   e

2
    a   b   c   d   e

3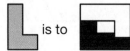
    a   b   c   d   e

Complete the following sequences.

4 _____ 3072 _____ 768 384 192 96

5 _____ $12\frac{1}{3}$ $13\frac{1}{2}$ $14\frac{2}{3}$ $15\frac{5}{6}$ _____ $18\frac{1}{6}$ $19\frac{1}{3}$

6 2.12 1.59 1.06 0.53 _____ −0.53 _____

7 6561 _____ 729 243 81 _____ 9

8 14.41 18.81 _____ _____ 32.01 36.41 40.81

Year 6 pupils were asked how many people lived in their home, including themselves. This chart shows the results. Use it to answer the following questions.

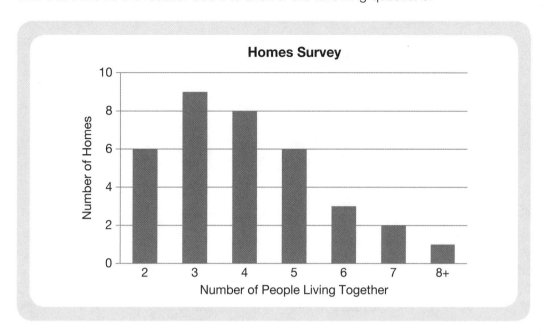

9 How many children are in Year 6? _____

10 What is the mode for the number of people living together? _____

11 How many children live in a house with more than four people? _____

There are 36 balls in a bag. Nine of them are blue, 12 of them are red and the rest are green. Answer with a fraction in its simplest form.

12 What is the probability of picking out a red ball? _____

13 What is the probability of picking out a blue ball? _____

14 How many balls are green? _____

Test 30: Sequences

Continue these sequences.

1 225   169   121   81   49   _____   _____

2 1   2   3   5   8   13   _____   _____

3 −1   −3   −9   −27   −81   −243   _____   _____

4 455   364   273   182   91   _____   _____

Complete these sequences.

5 2   3   5   7   _____   13   17   _____

6 −84   _____   −98   −105   _____   −119   −126

7 _____   0.02   0.4   8   160   3200   _____

8 _____   18.27   19.54   _____   22.08   23.35   24.62

Continue these sequences.

9 $\frac{1}{8}$ $\frac{3}{8}$ $\frac{5}{8}$ $\frac{7}{8}$ _____   _____

10 29.6   14.8   7.4   3.7   1.85   _____   _____

11 $2\frac{8}{9}$ _____ $4\frac{2}{3}$ $5\frac{5}{9}$ _____ $7\frac{1}{3}$ $8\frac{2}{9}$ $9\frac{1}{9}$

12 _____   11.68   9.36   7.04   4.72   2.4   0.08   _____

Test 31: **Data**

This is part of a train timetable. Use the table to answer the following questions.

	Train 1	Train 2	Train 3	Train 1	Train 2	Train 3
Bridgnorth	10:25	12:20	12:45	14:05	15:25	16:45
Hampton Loade	10:42	12:37		14:22	15:42	
Highley	10:52	12:48		14:33	15:52	
Arley	11:03	12:59		14:43	16:02	
Bewdley	11:18	13:14	13:20	14:59	16:17	17:20
Kidderminster	11:29	13:25	13:31	15:10	16:29	17:31

1 What is the shortest time to travel from Highley to Bewdley?

2 If I catch the 12:20 train, get off at Hampton Loade, spend an hour and a half there before continuing my journey to Kidderminster, what time will I reach Kidderminster?

3 If I catch the first train to Bewdley, spend two hours shopping and then get the next train to Kidderminster, what time will I reach Kidderminster?

4 If tickets from Bridgnorth to Kidderminster are £12.80 return for an adult, with a 50% discount for children, how much does it cost Mr and Mrs Vaughan and their three children to buy return tickets from Bridgnorth to Kidderminster?

5 Mr Vaughan travels from Bridgnorth to Kidderminster and back from Monday to Friday for 45 weeks of the year. An annual travel pass is £2500. How much will Mr Vaughan save if he buys a travel pass?

Time for a break! ★ Go to Puzzle Page 77 →

Test 32: Word Problems

Test time: 0 — 5 — 10 minutes

I bake a pizza that weighs 1.26 kg. Half of the mass of the pizza consists of the base and the remainder is topping. Of the topping, one third of the mass consists of tomato sauce. Of the remaining topping, 20% is mushroom, 30% is pineapple and the rest is onion. Underline the correct answer from options **a–e**.

1 How much does the tomato sauce weigh?

  a 850 g **b** 500 g **c** 630 g **d** 315 g **e** 210 g

2 How much does the pineapple weigh?

  a 500 g **b** 300 g **c** 150 g **d** 126 g **e** 30 g

Janice is decorating a cake for a party. The cake is 40 cm long, 45 cm wide and 6 cm tall. She wants to cover the whole cake except for the bottom. Janice then plans to decorate the top with marshmallows that are 2 cm square.

3 How much icing does Janice need?

  a 10 800 cm² **b** 4350 cm² **c** 2820 cm² **d** 1800 cm² **e** 760 cm²

4 How many whole marshmallows will she need to cover the top of the cake?

  a 4500 **b** 440 **c** 45 **d** 14 **e** 4

The scale of my map is 1 : 350 000.

5 I have to travel 70 km. How many centimetres will this be on the map?

  a 7 cm **b** 20 cm **c** 35 cm **d** 70 cm **e** 75 cm

6 On the map, the service station is 4 cm away from my destination. How many kilometres will this be?

  a 4 km **b** 10 km **c** 14 km **d** 40 km **e** 140 km

Test 33: **Word Problems**

Test time: 0 — 5 — 10 minutes

Mr Turley is buying some pencils and crayons for his pupils.
There are 30 pencils in a box and Mr Turley needs six boxes.
The crayons cost 27p each and Mr Turley needs 65 of them.
If he pays for these items with four £20 notes, he would get £19.25 change.

1 How much does one pencil cost? _____ [3]

2 Mr Turley sees that another brand of crayons has a special offer of 'Buy two, get one free'. They are also 27p each.

How much would 65 of these crayons cost him? _____ [3]

3 Mr Turley goes for this special offer along with the six boxes of pencils.

How much is his total bill? _____ [1]

Noah looks at the clothes in his wardrobe. He realises that $\frac{3}{4}$ of them are trousers and the remainder are tops. He notices that 20% of the trousers are jeans. He sees that of the tops, one in three of them have long sleeves and of these, half of them are hoodies. Noah has five hoodies.

4 How many items of clothing are there in Noah's wardrobe? _____ [2]

5 How many of Noah's clothes are jeans? _____ [2]

6 How many items of clothing are short-sleeved tops? _____ [2]

The train left the station with 482 passengers. At the first stop, 50% of the passengers got off and another 318 passengers got on. At the second stop, 383 passengers got on and 42 passengers got off. At the third stop, $\frac{1}{3}$ of the passengers got off and 400 passengers got on.

7 How many passengers were on the train as it left the second stop? _____ [1]

8 How many passengers were on the train as it left the third stop? _____ [1]

Total [15]

Test 34: Mixed

Captain Redbeard and his four rascal pirates are dividing up their 450 gold coins in the ratio 1:2:3:4:5 with Captain Redbeard taking the largest amount.

1 How many gold coins do they each get, smallest amount first?

_____

2 The pirates with the lowest two amounts pool their coins together and then steal the gold coins from Captain Redbeard before sharing the total amount between them. How many coins do they each have?

_____

3 Captain Redbeard is furious and takes the remaining gold coins from the other two pirates who didn't steal from him. How many gold coins does he now have?

_____

Complete these sequences.

4 1   10   3   20   5   30   7   40   _____   _____

5 7   99   14   88   _____   _____   28   66   35   55

6 _____   _____   132   26   120   39   108   52   96   65

7 15   240   _____   _____   45   60   60   30   75   15

8 17   105   34   84   51   _____   _____   42   85   21

9 80   80   40   100   20   120   10   _____   _____   160

Holly Hall School has a subsidised canteen. This is today's menu. Use it to answer the following questions.

Salad 49p	Chips 59p	Baked Potato 65p
Rice 30p	Peas 39p	Beans 35p
Burger 97p	Chilli £1.55	Lasagne £1.05

10 Ellie buys a burger, chips and beans. How much change does she get from £10?

11 Roisin buys lasagne, peas and salad. How much does she pay?

12 Philip buys chilli, rice and peas for himself and lasagne for his sister. How much change does he get from £20?

Which pattern on the right is a reflection of the pattern on the left?

13
              a   b   c   d   e

14
              a   b   c   d   e

15
              a   b   c   d   e

16
              a   b   c   d   e

Total 27

Test 35: **Non-verbal Reasoning**

Test time: 0   5   10 minutes

Which pattern completes the grid? Underline the correct answer.

1
                                           a   **b**   **c**   **d**   **e**

2
                                         a   **b**   **c**   **d**   **e**

3
                                         a   **b**   **c**   **d**   **e**

4
                                         a   **b**   **c**   **d**   **e**

5
                                         a   **b**   **c**   **d**   **e**

There is a set of pictures on the left with a missing picture shown by a question mark. Underline the correct option from the right to complete the set.

Test 36: Data

This table shows the price of items in a clothes retail outlet. The cost price is what the shop pays for buying the goods. The profit is a percentage of the cost price and is the money they make. The retail price is the cost price plus the profit added. The retailer has not had time to complete the retail price.

Item	Cost Price	Profit	Retail Price
School jumper	£6.00	60%	£9.60
School blouse	£2.50	50%	£
School blazer	£25.00	40%	£
School tie	£2.80	50%	£

1 Work out the retail price for each of the following items:

   a blouse _____   **b** blazer _____   **c** tie _____

Mrs Kapoor needs uniforms for her children. She buys one school jumper, two school blouses, one school blazer and one school tie.

2 What is the total cost price of her items? _____

3 What is the total retail price of her items? _____

Mrs Kapoor's sister is also buying uniforms for her children. She buys two school jumpers, five school blouses and one school tie.

4 What is the total cost price of her items? _____

5 What is the total retail price of her items? _____

6 How much profit does the shop make altogether on their sales to Mrs Kapoor and her sister? _____

This pie chart shows the type of breakfast cereal preferred by children at Hixon School. 240 children took part in the survey. Use the chart to answer the following questions.

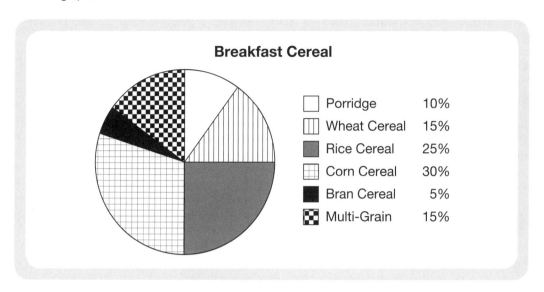

7 How many children preferred rice breakfast cereal? _____

8 How many children preferred either porridge or corn cereal? _____

9 How many children preferred multi-grain or wheat cereal? _____

10 How many children did not choose corn cereal? _____

11 Which type of breakfast cereal did 24 children choose? _____

12 Which type of breakfast cereal did 12 children choose? _____

Test 37: Word Problems

Richard buys a book costing £25, two pens at £3.60 each and some writing paper for £3.50. He uses two £20 notes to pay for them. He sees a pencil set on his way out of the shop reduced by 75% from £7 and goes back to buy it.

1 How much do the book, the pens and the writing paper cost altogether?

    a £71.40   **b** £35.70   **c** £28.96   **d** £14.60   **e** £34.70

2 How much change does Richard receive when paying for the book, the pens and the writing paper?

    a £24.30   **b** £14.30   **c** £14.60   **d** £2.76   **e** £4.30

3 How much does Richard pay for the set of pencils?

    a £7   **b** £6.30   **c** £3.50   **d** £1.75   **e** 75p

A car company has a production line making 1000 cars a week. Each week every 3rd car has a sun roof, every 10th car is white and every 12th car is fitted with a diesel engine.

4 How many cars are made each week that have a sunroof?

    a 334   **b** 333   **c** 332   **d** 300   **e** 30

5 How many cars have a diesel engine each week?

    a 833   **b** 830   **c** 83   **d** 80   **e** 8

6 How many cars are white and have a sun roof each week?

    a 33   **b** 330   **c** 38   **d** 380   **e** 100

George has bought some magazine subscriptions at discounted rates. The football magazine was originally £35.50 but has been reduced by £7.10 and a railway modelling magazine has been reduced by 30% from its original price of £51.00.

7 What is the percentage reduction in the cost of the football magazine?

    a 5%   **b** 10%   **c** 15%   **d** 20%   **e** 35%

8 What is the new cost of the railway modelling magazine?

    a £35.70   **b** £50   **c** £42.70   **d** £24.50   **e** £17.35

Test 38: Word Problems

Test time: 0   5   10 minutes

The journey from Whiston to Westry is 42 kilometres. The journey from Westry to Cam is 85 kilometres. The journey from Cam to Whiston is 62 kilometres. Underline the correct answer from options **a–e**.

1 Jenna drives from Whiston to Westry and spends $1\frac{1}{2}$ hours with friends before returning back to Whiston. She travels at 63 kilometres per hour on each journey. How long is her journey from Whiston to Westry?

   a 1 hour   **b** 50 minutes   **c** 40 minutes   **d** 30 minutes   **e** 20 minutes

2 If Jenna left home at 10:30 a.m., what time does she get back home?

   a 12:00 noon   **b** 12:30 p.m.   **c** 12:50 p.m.   **d** 1:10 p.m.   **e** 1:20 p.m.

3 Jason leaves the house at 10 a.m., drives from Whiston to Westry, spends 30 minutes at the doctor's, then drives on to Cam. After an hour of shopping, he returns back to Whiston. He travels at 63 kilometres per hour on each journey. At what time does Jason get home?

   a 1:00 p.m.   **b** 1:30 p.m.   **c** 2:00 p.m.   **d** 2:30 p.m.   **e** 3:30 p.m.

Four girls are rehearsing their piece of music. Zara hits a drum every six minutes. Dora hits a wood block every three minutes. Melody hits a triangle every four minutes and Evie hits a tambourine every 12 minutes. The four girls begin hitting their instruments together at 10:00 a.m. and continue their pattern until 11:00 a.m.

4 At what time do Zara and Dora next hit their instrument at the same time?

   a 10:02   **b** 10:03   **c** 10:04   **d** 10:05   **e** 10:06

5 At what time do all four girls next hit their instrument at the same time?

   a 10:06   **b** 10:08   **c** 10:12   **d** 10:20   **e** 10:24

6 How many times do all four girls hit their instrument at the same time in the hour?

   a 4   **b** 5   **c** 6   **d** 10   **e** 12

Total   10

Test 39: **Mixed**

Martha needs to purchase a new garden fence. Company A offers a deluxe fence at £2100, company B has a standard fence at £1250 and company C say they can offer a similar fence for £990. Each company is keen to provide Martha's fence and offer the following discounts: Company A a 33% discount, Company B a £400 reduction and Company C a 15% reduction.

1 What is the discounted price that Company A is now offering? _____

2 What is the amount of money that Company C is willing to take off? _____

3 What is the percentage decrease in the cost of the fence from Company B? _____

This table shows the scores that three girls achieved when they used a spinner eight times. Jess spun an eight-sided spinner, Elle spun a six-sided spinner and Lili spun a four-sided spinner.

Jess		Elle		Lili	
8	2	3	1	1	4
6	8	3	3	4	2
1	4	5	6	1	3
3	8	2	3	3	2

4 One of the spinners is biased. Which do you think it is most likely to be? How do you know?

_____

_____

_____

5 What was the mean average score for Jess?

_____

Rita uses the following recipe for baking cakes. It makes 18 small cakes.

Recipe: Small cakes
From the kitchen of: **Rita**

Ingredients:
100 g self-raising flour
100 g sugar
100 g butter
3 eggs
75 g sultanas
1 teaspoon milk

6 How much self-raising flour will Rita need if she bakes 45 cakes? _____

7 How many eggs will Rita need if she bakes 66 cakes? _____

8 If Rita uses 350 g of sugar, how many cakes will this make? _____

9 If Rita uses 1125 g of sultanas, how many cakes will this make? _____

Complete these sequences. Underline the correct answer from options **a–e**.

10 718.93   719.38   719.83   720.28   _____   721.18

a 720.03   b 720.63   c 720.73   d 720.83   e 721.03

11 _____   51.031   52.741   54.451   56.161   57.871

a 49.321   b 49.851   c 50.941   d 50.321   e 50.871

12 15.95   31.9   63.8   127.6   255.2   _____

a 520.4   b 500.2   c 510.2   d 500.4   e 510.4

Test 40: **Mixed**

Which cube cannot be made from the given net? Underline the correct answer.

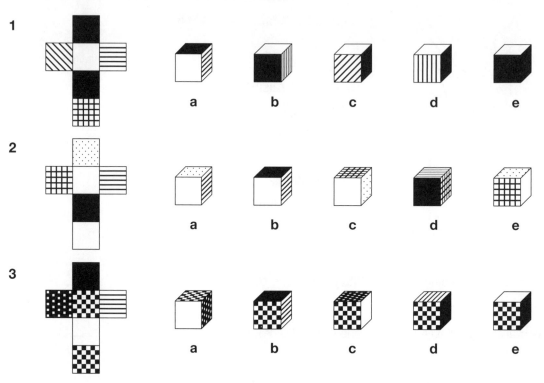

1   a   b   c   d   e

2   a   b   c   d   e

3   a   b   c   d   e

Which shape on the right is a 3D rotation of the shape on the left? Underline the correct answer.

4

   a   b   c   d   e

5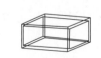

   a   b   c   d   e

6

   a   b   c   d   e

Richard buys 120 apples for £16.80. He sells them on a market stall for 38p each. He also sells bags of five apples for £1.50.

7 How much profit can Richard make if he sells all of the apples as single pieces of fruit?

    a £28.80   **b** £45.60   **c** £16.80   **d** £7.50   **e** £5.00

8 How much profit can Richard make if he sells all of the apples as bags of five?

    a £36.00   **b** £19.20   **c** £16.00   **d** £8.50   **e** £5.00

9 Richard sells ten bags of apples and the remaining apples as single items. How much profit does he make?

    a £86.00   **b** £41.60   **c** £26.60   **d** £17.50   **e** £24.80

There are 15 candles in a pack. There are 14 packs in a box. There are 40 boxes in a crate and there are three crates in the shop.

10 How many candles are there in the shop?

    a 550 000   **b** 5202   **c** 252   **d** 2520   **e** 25 200

11 The shop sells the candles for 12p each. How much money will the shop get if they sell half of their stock?

    a £20 120   **b** £2012   **c** £1512   **d** £152   **e** £151

Complete the following sequences.

12 13.81   14.7   15.59   _____   17.37   18.26   _____

13 $1\frac{2}{3}$ $1\frac{3}{5}$ $1\frac{8}{15}$ _____   _____ $1\frac{1}{3}$ $1\frac{4}{15}$

Time for a break! ★ *Go to Puzzle Page 79* →

Total   21

Puzzle 1

Paper Punching Problems

These sheets of paper have been folded and then a paper punch stamps holes in the paper. If you open up the paper, which one is the correct pattern? Underline the correct answer.

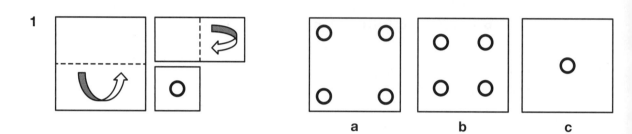

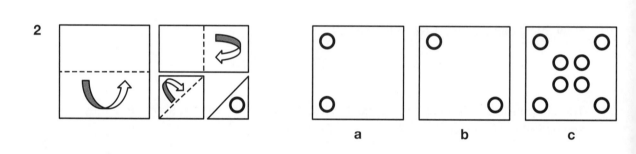

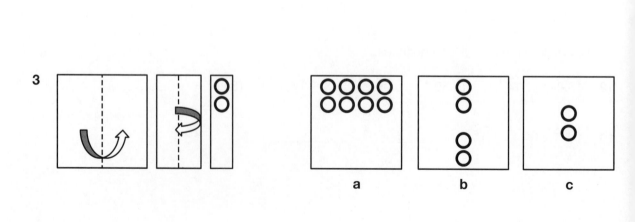

Puzzle 2

Locked Doors

Every door has a key that fits and every key has a tag. There is a fraction on each door, a decimal number on each key and a percentage on each tag. Join each door to the key and tag that have equivalent values.

Puzzle 3

Grid Lock

Each of the number grids below has some numbers missing. Complete the grid by filling in the missing numbers:

×	16	17	18
13		221	234
14	224	238	
15	240		270

×	1.4	3.2	2.5
7.2		23.04	18
8.6	12.04		21.5
9.1	12.74	29.12	

+	65.29		5.001
0.92	66.21	32.16	5.921
47.692	112.982	78.932	
12.21		43.45	17.211

Puzzle 4

Secret Codes

The alphabet has been written out in code. Work out the code and then unlock each secret message.

A	B	C	D	E	F	G	H	I	J	K	L	M
4												

N	O	P	Q	R	S	T	U	V	W	X	Y	Z
												3

11	8	15	15	18

11	4	25	8

2	18	24

22	18	15	25	8	7

23	11	12	22

2	8	23

Now try writing another message using the same code.

Puzzle 5

Robot Treasures

There are three robots who have buried their treasure. Follow the directions for each robot to find the treasure.

Robot 1: Begin on (7, 3). Move north 5 cells, east 6 cells, south-west 2 cells, west 10 cells.

Where is the treasure? _____

Robot 2: Begin on (12, 10). Move south 8 cells, west 7 cells, north-east 6 cells.

Where is the treasure? _____

Robot 3: Begin on (2, 1). Move north-east 10 cells, west 5 cells, south 4 cells, west 5 cells, south 3 cells.

Where is the treasure? _____

Puzzle 6

Shaping Space For Sheep

Farmer Hoskins has four fields and 192 sheep. Put the correct number of sheep in each field using the information below to help.

Field 1
- Can only hold a number of sheep that is a square number.
- Holds exactly $\frac{1}{4}$ of the number of sheep as Field 2 and exactly $\frac{1}{3}$ of the number of sheep as Field 3.

How many sheep? _____

Field 2
- Can only hold a number of sheep that is a cube number.
- Can only hold an even number of sheep.

How many sheep? _____

Field 3
- Holds exactly $\frac{3}{4}$ of the number of sheep as Field 2.
- Can only hold a number of sheep that is in the 6 times table.

How many sheep? _____

Field 4
- Holds exactly the same number of sheep as half of the other fields added together.
- Is an even number.

How many sheep? _____

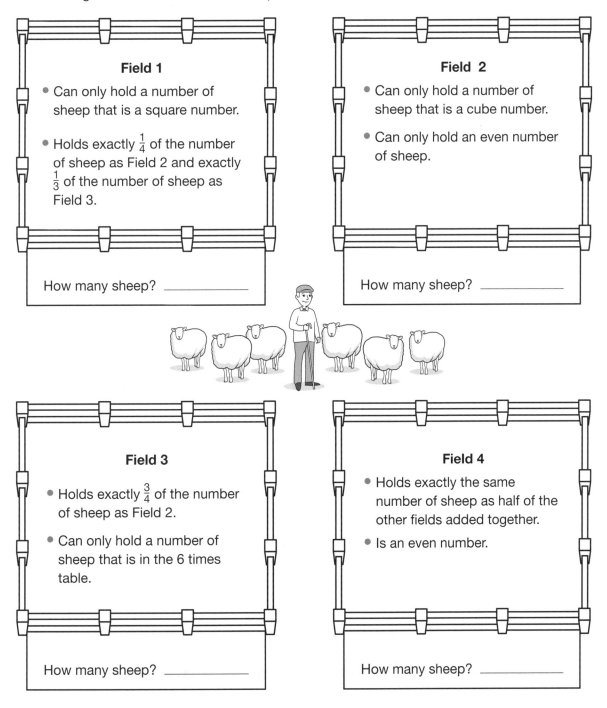

Puzzle 7

Number Riddles

Find a number that matches these clues:

1 I am a factor of 72.

2 I am a square number.

3 One of my digits is a prime number.

What am I?

---

1 I am a cube number.

2 I am a multiple of 3.

3 I am a four-figure number and my 1st and 2nd digits are the same.

4 I am a multiple of 5.

What am I?

---

1 I am a triangular number.

2 I am a factor of 168.

3 I am a multiple of 7.

4 I am an odd number.

What am I?

Puzzle 8

Clever Conundrum

Here is a table for a list of places. Work out in which order the places need to be positioned using the clues given:

	Places
1	
2	
3	
4	
5	
6	
7	
8	
9	
10	
11	
12	

Clues:

Birmingham's position is a factor of 12 and an odd number.

Chester's position is a cubed number.

Durham's position is a square number.

Exeter's position is a prime number.

Gloucester's position and the sides of a kite share this number.

Leed's position is written as X in Roman numerals.

Liverpool's position is a triangular number.

London's position is written as a V in Roman numerals.

Manchester's position is an even prime number.

Norwich's position is written as I in Roman numerals.

Stafford's position can also be called a dozen.

York's position has a times table that begins with digits that are the same.

Progress chart

How did you do? Fill in your score below and shade in the corresponding boxes to compare your progress across the different tests.

	50%	100%		50%	100%

Test 1, p2 Score: ____ /13

Test 2, p4 Score: ____ /13

Test 3, p6 Score: ____ /13

Test 4, p7 Score: ____ /12

Test 5, p8 Score: ____ /13

Test 6, p10 Score: ____ /12

Test 7, p12 Score: ____ /12

Test 8, p14 Score: ____ /11

Test 9, p15 Score: ____ /17

Test 10, p16 Score: ____ /12

Test 11, p18 Score: ____ /13

Test 12, p20 Score: ____ /24

Test 13, p21 Score: ____ /15

Test 14, p22 Score: ____ /12

Test 15, p24 Score: ____ /16

Test 16, p26 Score: ____ /24

Test 17, p27 Score: ____ /9

Test 18, p28 Score: ____ /12

Test 19, p30 Score: ____ /20

Test 20, p32 Score: ____ /9

Test 21, p34 Score: ____ /12

Test 22, p35 Score: ____ /17

Test 23, p36 Score: ____ /9

Test 24, p46 Score: ____ /18

Test 25, p48 Score: ____ /13

Test 26, p50 Score: ____ /16

Test 27, p51 Score: ____ /9

Test 28, p52 Score: ____ /10

Test 29, p54 Score: ____ /19

Test 30, p56 Score: ____ /24

Test 31, p57 Score: ____ /9

Test 32, p58 Score: ____ /11

Test 33, p59 Score: ____ /15

Test 34, p60 Score: ____ /27

Test 35, p62 Score: ____ /9

Test 36, p64 Score: ____ /18

Test 37, p66 Score: ____ /14

Test 38, p67 Score: ____ /10

Test 39, p68 Score: ____ /22

Test 40, p70 Score: ____ /21